The Future of Social Work

Terry Bamford

M

MACMILLAN

First published 1990

Published by
MACMILLAN EDUCATION LTD
Houndmills, Basingstoke, Hampshire RG21 2XS
and London
Companies and representatives
throughout the world

Typeset by Footnote Graphics,
Warminister, Wilts

Printed in Hong Kong

British Library Cataloguing in Publication Data
Bamford, Terry
The future of social work
1. Great Britain. Welfare work
I. Title
361.3'0941
ISBN 0–333–46396–X (hardcover)
ISBN 0–333–46397–8 (paperback)

The Future of Social Work

Also by Terry Bamford

Managing Social Work

To my parents and grandparents

Contents

Acknowledgements

Writing a book is a very personal undertaking but in the process one incurs many debts of gratitude. The initial idea for a book which would both look forward but set that in the context of recent social work history came from Jo Campling and Steven Kennedy. I am grateful to them for their encouragement, continuing support and wise counsel as the book took shape.

The ideas were shaped by many individuals who unwittingly provided stimulus and inspiration. Two in particular deserve special recognition. Joan Cooper provided detailed and helpful comments which were invaluable. Stuart Etherington's robust enthusiasm for the development of welfare pluralism was invigorating. Without knowing it he provided the spur to put pen to paper.

Participation is a recurrent theme of the book. I have greatly valued the opportunity to be involved in active creative and thoughtful professional associations like BASW and ADSS and that too has influenced my thinking.

The staff of the Southern Health and Social Services Board have provided me with the opportunity to explore new ideas, and have consistently displayed an openness to innovation and a creativity which represents all that is best in social work. To all of them I am grateful. To my patient secretary, Anne Nethercote, go my special thanks for her help in getting the manuscript into a legible state.

The author and publishers acknowledge with thanks the permission of CCETSW to reproduce Figure 4.1 and of the Audit Commission to reproduce Figure 5.1 and Table 5.1 from *Making Reality of Community Care*.

Finally but most important of all I thank my family – Margaret, Andrew and Sarah – for their patience, forbearance and encouragement without which the book would never have been completed.

TERRY BAMFORD

Foreword

Anyone rash enough to take as a title *The Future of Social Work* invites the response that there should be a question mark after the title. Twenty years after the Seebohm Report social work has failed to establish its independent professional status, has a basic training shorter than that of the other occupational groups involved in community care, and has dropped precipitately in public esteem. Its organisational future too is uncertain, threatened by the Government's unremitting hostility to local government.

It is hard now to remember the sense of optimism, the belief in the capacity of social work to make a real impact on the lives of the vulnerable, disadvantaged, and disturbed, that characterised the time between the publication of the Seebohm Report and the advent of social services departments. Scotland had moved earlier with the creation of social work departments, and organisational change seemed to promise both an increase in resources for social care and a commitment to combating deprivation.

What went wrong? How did that rich promise so swiftly become tarnished? What lessons can be drawn from the recent history of social work in Britain? To influence the future it is first necessary to understand the past. The collective memory of social work is notoriously short and its pursuit of currently fashionable nostrums correspondingly uncritical. A sense of history is a useful corrective to such ephemeral enthusiasms.

The history offered here is brief and selective. It focuses upon the years following the publication of the Seebohm Report because they marked a turning-point in the scale of social welfare provision and established the framework for contemporary social work and its organisation. By identifying emerging trends in practice and organisation, and by a study of the sometimes opaque pattern of Government thinking, one can begin to construct a view of the likely future.

The view offered is a personal view. By the date of publication some of the issues canvassed may be on the way to resolution but the focus of the book is on those issues where change takes decades rather than months. These are the relevance of structure and organisation both to public perception and professional satisfaction, the lack of a strong professional identity in social work, and the implications of consumerism for the future provision of social work.

Size and Structure

There was a common strand in social policy developments when the Seebohm Report was published, and in the years of its implementation. It was the shared belief that bigger meant better, whether in the creation of super-ministries at Governmental level, the reorganisation of local government and its services or the restructuring of industry. Economies of scale would produce greater efficiency. Large-scale enterprises would attract and retain talent. In social work the initial reorganisation in 1971 into multipurpose departments was succeeded by the 1974 reorganisation of local government, further compounding the move to large-scale units of organisation.

The effects on social work have been predominantly negative. While there have been significant advances in resource provision, these have been concentrated in residential and day care services. Those services most visible to the consumer – fieldwork and domiciliary services – have not expanded as rapidly. Nearly twenty years after the first unified departments came into being, 'the welfare' is still more real to many clients than the designation 'social services'. And both share the characteristic of an impersonal bureaucratic machine over which clients exercise little influence.

The turnover of staff, the layers of managerial control and the absence of clearly-identified personal responsibility have combined to create a sense of public unease about the effectiveness of welfare provision. That has been reinforced by the highly publicised child-care tragedies and the failure of successive inquiries to produce a scapegoat to satisfy the public's concern. The reporting of these cases has tended to confirm and reinforce the stereotype of self-protective structures in which responsibility is blurred. Paradoxically that perception is shared by many within social work who regret the decline in personal accountability, and see the structures of social services departments as stifling creativity, initiative and good practice.

The lack of a practitioner career structure within social work reflects the differential values accorded to skilled practice and managerial responsibility. It means that the most able practitioners are promoted away from client contact as organisational imperatives are accorded precedence over the quality of service enjoyed by individual clients.

Redressing the problems created by size will be a preoccupation of the nineties. At one extreme are the radical prescriptions of the ideologues of the market, who would cheerfully see the dismemberment of direct public sector provision and the emergence of a host of competing providers. Such diversity, while addressing the issues of impersonal bureaucracy, would produce other problems in terms of duplication, overlapping provision and geographical variations in volume and quality of service. At the other extreme, those who foresee a continuation of the existing or even enhanced role of social services departments acknowledge the importance of improving access, communication and consultation for and with clients.

An Uncertain Profession

The implementation of the Seebohm recommendations should have been the launch-pad for a consolidation of the social work profession. Instead, the failure of social work to achieve its professional aspirations of self-regulation in terms of training and disciplinary action against professional failings encapsulated the failure of social work as a whole to reach agreement on its role and function.

The social work strikes in 1977 and 1978 epitomised the dilemma. In pursuance of a grievance related to pay and conditions, social workers took strike action in a significant number of local authorities. Their actions did little damage to the employing authorities and the damage to clients was hard to identify or quantify. The action was most effective in its symbolic repudiation of traditional concepts of professionalism based on the primacy of service to clients.

There is in social work a widespread agreement about the irrelevance of models of professionalism based on the established professions of the law and medicine. The commitment of social workers to change in society and to redressing the inequalities and injustices which they see daily leads to justified anger at the deficiencies of existing social systems. Anger, however, is no substitute for thought. Too often social workers have substituted the emotional spasm of solidarity with the working class for careful analysis. Political identity has been more important than professional identity.

Two examples of this tendency can be offered – both have operated to the detriment of social work's attempt to establish its role in society. First, there is a deeply ingrained ambivalence about training and qualifications even among those who possess them or teach on courses which provide them. It finds expression in suspicion of 'elitism', in a repudiation of the view that some can be better equipped by training and experience to fulfil social work roles than others with a kindly disposition but lacking formal qualifications. This is a spurious egalitarianism which has consistently undermined the admittedly half-hearted attempts of the Central Council for Education and Training in Social Work to establish a graduated hierarchy of qualifications.

Second, some social workers believe that the task of social control is not one for social workers but for the police. The reality is, however, that social workers as employees of the state are employed to undertake specific tasks. Unarticulated but implicit in that employment is the belief of the employers that the provision of welfare services is a contributory factor to the maintenance of public stability. When social workers become involved with the mentally-disordered individual presenting florid symptoms, or the disturbed adolescent, or the child at risk, they are not acting as the representatives of the altruistic impulses of society. They are being paid to quieten the situation, to relieve anxiety, and to exercise some control over a situation in which the normal mechanisms of control had broken down. There is nothing dishonourable about an honest recognition that social workers are in a social control role. The difficulties come when that reality is denied as if social workers were indeed a self-regulating group of independent contractors. Asserting a higher professional obligation to the welfare of the client is untenable if the other indicators of professional status are absent.

These self-contradictory attitudes are widely held and have contributed to the inability of the British Association of Social Workers to exercise a major role over the development of social work in Britain. There are some grounds for suggesting that the 1990s will see a reversion to professionalism. First the far more differentiated employment market likely to emerge in an age of welfare pluralism will break the power of local authorities as virtual monopolistic providers of social work employment. As employers local authorities have been as hostile to the development of a vigorous independent professionalism as have trade unions. The erosion of their influence and the desire of employees in small welfare agencies to have an external reference point for good practice may lead to a resurgence of interest in professional bodies, as happened in the USA with the decline in public sector provision and the development of alternative providers.

Second, the closer linkages with health care workers will focus attention on the anomalous position of social work as the lone skilled occupational group without some form of registration and quality control. Third, the demographic shift now taking place, with the decline in the working population, will force social work into a role orchestrating support workers of various kinds. There will not be sufficient staff available of the calibre required to maintain present employment patterns.

The response which social work makes to these trends will depend on the degree to which it can incorporate the values being expressed under the banner of consumerism.

The New Consumerism

Consumerism is one of those rare concepts that does not automatically carry a political label of Right or Left. The emphasis on freedom of choice is appealing to the Right, the extension of user power is attractive to the Left. Yet despite the calls in both the Seebohm and Barclay Reports for greater attention to ways in which the community could be involved in personal social services, relatively little has been achieved in shifting the balance of power between providers of service and consumers.

There are some hopeful signs in shifts which have begun to take root in recent years. The development of increased client-access to files, the emphasis on parental rights to information and to be heard in case-conferences affecting their children's future, moves to decentralise services and to secure community participation, the growth of advocacy schemes offering a voice to those who have been powerless, legislative provision strengthening the rights of carers to be consulted – and the growing acceptance of the concept that services are a right and not in the discretionary gift of the provider, are indicative of a major paradigm shift from the producer-orientation which has hitherto dominated the welfare services.

Some of those changes have been enthusiastically espoused by social workers. Others have been viewed with suspicion as making the already difficult task of the worker even more complex. The future of social work is critically dependent on its ability and readiness to harness the new consumerism and to work with it. In assessing whether this is likely to occur, it is important to go back to the basic values of social work and test them against the demands of a consumer orientation. What one finds is a striking congruence between the long-established value statements of the profession expressed in Codes of Ethics and the aspirations of the contemporary consumer.

The concept of citizenship is one which directs attention to the rights of clients as fellow-citizens. The social worker respecting those rights has to ensure that the clients have full access to all relevant information, are aware of rights to see the case record, to register complaints, and to appeal against decisions. The concept of empowerment is not new. It is firmly enshrined in the notion of client self-determination which has been a central social work value for half a century. What is new is the increased readiness of social workers to give reality to what was formerly an abstract principle. If this can be further developed, the transfer of power and responsibility to service-users may constitute a professional radicalism far more persuasive and influential on clients' lives than the blind alley of a political radicalism has proved.

One of the challenges facing all welfare services will be the establishment of appropriate skills, knowledge and structures to deliver effective services to ethnic minorities. Participation of minorities and real control in shaping those services is essential if the concept of citizenship is to be non-racist.

While the future holds uncertainties and the likelihood of major change, it is not a prospect which need be feared by social workers. The consumerist thrust of current developments has to be matched by a new professionalism, emphasising rights and power for clients. While there is a latent tension between social control and empowerment this will be eased by the development of more differentiated patterns of employment. The values of social work, which have been too long been subjugated by the dominant role of the employing agency, will again mould a practice which is flexible, creative and fulfilling. Romantic nonsense? Maybe so, but the future is not predetermined. It will be influenced by those bold enough to look beyond immediate time horizons and able to convey a vision of the future they want to achieve. Hitherto, social work, preoccupied with present problems, has failed to do so. This book is a modest contribution to that endeavour.

1

A Turbulent Environment

It is tempting to look back at social work practice in the years before the Seebohm Report (1968) as an age of innocence. Social work was delivered in a variety of agencies usually serving specific client groups. Its practice reflected a growing sense of professional unity and a developing self-confidence in the ability of social work to bring about positive change both in the lives of individuals and in wider society. It enjoyed public approval as a necessary part of welfare provision. The reality for clients was different, as the picture of patchy, uncoordinated and under-resourced services drawn in the Report shows.

Contemporary social work is still in many ways the child of the Seebohm Report. Its organisational structure, its practice and its relationships with other agencies bear the hallmark of Seebohm. The measure of the change in public, professional and political attitudes can be seen in the context of the implementation of the Report and its recommendations and the gradual development of a challenge to the Report's assumptions.

Within ten years of the introduction of social services departments, Brewer and Lait asked in a trenchant critique, *Can Social Work Survive?* (1980). Their question reflected a growing scepticism about the validity of social work's claims to special skills and knowledge. At the time of publication their polemic attracted little support. The subsequent sustained criticism, initially linked to failings of individual practice in child-care tragedies, has changed the nature of public debate by challenging the very validity of social work.

The troubled environment in which social workers have to operate today is difficult and uncertain. Yet there is a striking consistency in the preoccupations of social work since the

1

Seebohm Report changed the face of the personal social services. There are lessons to be learned from the mistakes of the past twenty years in dealing with those preoccupations. The ability to avoid those mistakes in the future is critical if social work is to break free of its nostalgia for the collectivist solutions of the Welfare State and to adapt itself to the looser, more entrepreneurial structures now required.

The Personal Social Services

Unlike the health service or education, the personal social services are rarely the subject of everyday discussion. The failings of social services staff in one authority serving one client group may well attract attention, but the disparate activities covered by the personal social services lack any clear focus or identity. As Townsend pointed out at the time of the Seebohm Report, the personal social services were not drawn together until a quarter of a century after the postwar development of the education, housing, health and income maintenance services (Townsend 1970). Yet while social services departments may be the main agents for delivering personal social services, there are, too, numerous voluntary organisations and community groups, self-help organisations and charities, which contribute to the full range of personal social services.

The major recommendation of the Seebohm Report was the creation of a unified social service department drawing together the compartmentalised specialist services which had existed formerly, leading to a lack of coordination between agencies and problems of access for the client. The recommendation was warmly supported by the social work profession, which was developing a strong sense of identity. The first generic social work course in Britain and the establishment of the Standing Conference of Organisations of Social Workers had reflected the belief that 'social workers of all kinds have increasingly come to realise that they are dealing not with specific problems or handicaps but with people, and not with people in isolation but with people in a social situation, particularly in a family situation. All social work has therefore tended to become family social work.' (SCOSW 1965). In Britain the Seebohm Report seemed to capture that new thinking just as had the earlier Kilbrandon Report in Scotland.

Besides the structural change, Seebohm was an enthusiastic advocate of the social work role with communities and the potential for harnessing neighbourhood resources in the service of the community. Experiments with volunteers were given authoritative endorsement. This aspect of the Report received less attention than had been anticipated as the new departments had too many preoccupations with their own problems to develop a true community-orientated practice. The Barclay Report in 1982 is strikingly similar to Seebohm in its enthusiasm for community social work.

Organisational solutions were still viewed as an effective answer to the problems of human need, but the aftermath of implementation produced chaos rather than clarity as services with unequal resources, unequal supplies of trained staff and uneven professional standards were fused. The fledgling departments were obliged to grapple with a new legislative framework with the 1968 Health Services and Public Health Act, the 1969 Children and Young Persons Act, and the 1970 Chronically Sick and Disabled Persons Act. The implementation of the Seebohm recommendations and their impact on personal social services have been well described elsewhere (Cooper 1983; Hall 1976). The pace of expansion, with double-figure annual growth rates, meant that there was little opportunity for consolidation of experience and the development of skill. And just when a period of stability might have been anticipated, a further round of local government reorganisation in England and Wales in 1974 and in Scotland in 1975 set the whole process in motion again.

'The Party's Over'

For social work, the party had ended before Tony Crosland, Secretary of State for the Environment, called an end in 1975 to the untrammelled expansion of local government. It ended in January 1973 when an 8-year-old girl, Maria Colwell, died of injuries inflicted by her stepfather. Social work had to develop a thick skin to cope with the seemingly unending succession of child-care tragedies, each of which has brought in its wake attacks on the values and philosophy of social work practice and its ineffectiveness.

There were three reasons for the profound emotional impact of the Colwell case on the profession. First, it was the first such case and the face of 8-year-old Maria stared poignantly at readers of every daily paper. Secondly, it was dealt with by a full-scale public inquiry, with the consequence that the social worker most directly involved had to push her way into the hearing through a crowd of jeering, abusive onlookers. Thirdly, it marked the end of the honeymoon period when the effectiveness of social work as a means of changing human behaviour had been taken as axiomatic. The 1969 Children and Young Persons Act in England, the expansion of local authority services, and the beneficent effects assumed to flow from these changes were for the first time called into question. The scars left by the Colwell case on the collective psyche of social work have never fully healed as each year has brought a further reminder that social work decisions are rarely clear-cut, and that social workers are brokers in shades of grey, often seeking the lesser of two evils for those with whom they work.

The squeeze on public expenditure which commenced in 1975 hit social services hard. Growth had been exceptional even by the relaxed climate of the time with real growth of over 19 per cent in 1973/1974. The Labour Government in 1974 was confronted with rising levels of inflation, a huge public sector borrowing requirement, and a loss of international financial confidence. Soon after implementing a series of costly electoral commitments, it was obliged to retrench. The growth rate for personal social services was reduced to 2 per cent, sufficient to cope with the increased numbers of elderly people but allowing little room for expansion of any other services.

The language of reduced growth rates is that of politicians. To the public and to professionals they were cuts. There were cuts in planned day centres, homes and hostels as the capital programme bore the brunt of the reductions. But there were also cuts in the level of service as expectations were reined back, and departments confronted the necessity to switch resources from one sector to another. It was a rude interruption to the halcyon years of growth, and at first it was viewed as that – an interruption which would be followed by a resumption of expansion. That rosy assumption was dissipated by the publication in 1976 of *Priorities for Health and Personal Social Services* (DHSS 1976), an explicit recognition that for the foreseeable future departments would have to identify priorities, manage within limited resources, and effect change by switching resources within existing budgets.

Priorities

There is a contemporary ring to the priorities set by central government in 1976 – a commitment to community care through expansion of homes and hostels for the mentally ill and mentally handicapped, the development of domiciliary and day care services to enable people to remain at home rather than utilise places in residential care or hospitals, and an emphasis on joint planning with the health service as the means of making best use of scarce resources. Joint finance was introduced to oil the wheels of the transition to community care – from modest beginnings this grew to a sum equivalent to 4 per cent of all personal social services spending. The device of earmarking health service resources for personal social services expenditure which would benefit the health service, was greeted with initial scepticism, but turned out to be a fertile source of innovation and a necessary spur to joint work between the two agencies.

The way in which local authorities tackled the task of setting priorities is worth consideration for it conditioned both the approach to the cuts in real terms demanded by the Conservative Government in 1979 and to the interface with health service planning. The initial formulation in the 1974 Rate Fund Expenditure Circular was more specific than subsequent guidance. It identified:

(a) children at risk of ill-treatment
(b) the very elderly or severely handicapped living alone – especially those recently discharged from hospital, recently bereaved or in inadequate housing
(c) the mentally handicapped or mentally ill in urgent need of residential or day care, or domiciliary support, to prevent deterioration in their condition or to relieve intolerable strain on their families

(d) vulnerable individuals, or families with vulnerable members, who are at imminent risk of breakdown under severe stress imposed on them by handicap, illness, homelessness or poverty.

(DHSS 1974)

Unfortunately such guidance identified virtually all the clients of personal social services as priorities, and was of little practical assistance. The 1976 Priorities paper did differentiate between the client groups, giving priority weighting to primary care and to services for the elderly and handicapped, particularly the mentally disordered. Five years later *Care In Action* (DHSS 1981) continued the policy of identifying priority groups – the elderly, mentally ill, mentally handicapped, and the physically and sensorily handicapped – and priority services – those related to the care of children at risk and to the care and treatment of young offenders. Again the document was silent on those services which should be reduced to effect redeployment to these priorities.

In this policy vacuum a number of local authorities attempted to formulate criteria for the provision of service. The legal basis of intervention, the vulnerability of the client, the likelihood of an enforced change of residence, and the probable effectiveness of social work intervention were among the factors which figured in various systems. A more detailed discussion may be read elsewhere (Algie and Miller 1976; Bamford 1982; Whitmore and Fuller 1980), but few of the systems had a lasting impact on practice. Instead useful concepts were absorbed into the allocation systems used by team leaders.

The focus on priorities meant a constant search for ways of delivering services at lower cost. The ugly word 'substitutability' was used to describe the concept, which included the substitution of care in the community for costly acute hospital care, the transfer of patients from long-stay hospitals to community settings, the provision of intensive domiciliary support for those at risk of residential care, the development of low-cost day care rather than fully-staffed day centres, and the utilisation where possible of voluntary organisations and volunteers to undertake tasks carried out normally by full-time staff.

The concept of substitution drew together adherents from a number of perspectives. The mental health lobby welcomed the idea of community care, seeing it as less restrictive and depersonalising than care in large institutions. Improved quality of life for clients was seen as a desirable result of substitution. To the accountants community care was seen as a more cost-effective means of delivering services with a subsidy from social security funding. Those hostile to public sector bureaucracies saw the possibility of creating a plural system of welfare as a check to the monopoly power of social services by developing the role of voluntary organisations.

Some forms of substitutability are good professional practice. The rethinking of residential child care may have been precipitated by the high cost of placements in community homes with education on the premises, but it has led to a clarity of purpose and focus in intermediate treatment and residential care which has been wholly beneficial. While fostering is not a direct substitute for residential provision, it has benefited from the emphasis on community services.

Underlying the shift to community care was a somewhat naive view that it was cheaper to look after people in their own homes than in institutional settings. The true costs of community care are not easily calculated for they are spread across a number of different agencies. Those in the community receive health care from a GP and community nursing services; they are often in receipt of social security funding which may be substantial if they live in a home or hostel; and they may receive social services help through day care, domiciliary services or aids to daily living, sometimes free and sometimes with a charge being levied.

Informal Care

Community care has been an aspiration of social policy since the 1959 White Paper on Mental Health, but there has rarely been agreement about its meaning. Indeed it means different things for different client groups. For the long-stay mentally handicapped person it means life in a hostel or at home rather than in hospital, for children it means living at home or with foster-parents rather than in a children's home, for the elderly it means domiciliary support to remain at home rather than face a future of residential care or hospitalisation. At its crudest it means anywhere outside hospital. Part of the difficulty with the concept is that it is ever-changing. The

emphasis has switched from care in the community to care by the
community with increasing emphasis on the importance of informal care. It is a matter for political judgement whether this
recognition is the result of the work of Bayley (1982), Hadley and
McGrath (1980) and others or whether it reflects a desire to reduce
public expenditure on formal services.

There has been a congruence between the explicit desire of
government to cut spending, expressed most clearly in the 1979
Public Expenditure White Paper which called for cuts of 6.7 per
cent in personal social services spending in 1980/1981 and a strand
of academic writing on informal care. Hadley and Hatch, in a
powerful attack on the ineffectiveness of public bureaucracies,
baldly entitled *Social Welfare and the Failure of the State* (1981)
argued that the emphasis on centralised collectivist solutions to
social problems had created a number of shared assumptions.
Among these were:

1 The desirability of standard packages for application throughout the country.
2 That major changes in services should be planned and organised by central government.
3 That larger organisations are more likely to be efficient than
  small organisations through economies of scale, and superior
  ability to recruit and retain high-calibre staff.
4 That the consumer's voice in the management of services
  should be marginal, with primary public accountability
  through representative bodies.
5 That major organisational changes can be successfully designed and implemented without prior testing on a smaller
  scale.

These assumptions, they argued, served to insulate managers and
professionals from the demands and criticisms of consumers.

Hadley's views were reflected in the Barclay Report which laid
great emphasis on developing a community approach utilising the
resources of informal caring networks, and asserted, 'if social
work policy and practice were directed more to the support and
strengthening of informal networks, to caring for the carers and
less to the rescue of casualties when networks fail, it is likely that
the need for such referrals would be reduced' (Barclay 1982,

p. 200). Few would disagree with the importance of supporting
carers, but there is an important difference between care in and
care by the community. The wholly legitimate professional emphasis on finding better ways of helping carers through respite
schemes, improved day care and supportive networks can – if not
reflected in resources which provide real choice for carers – lead to
exploitation of informal care, and particularly of women, who are
usually the primary carers.

Barclay

The publication of the Barclay Report in 1982 followed a period of
professional soul-searching about the future direction of social
work practice. The introduction to the Report expressed it clearly:
'social workers find it difficult to come to terms with the complex
pressures which surround them. There is confusion about the
direction in which they are going and unease about what they
should be doing and the way in which they are organised and
deployed' (Barclay 1982, p. vii). The growth of social services and
social work departments meant that they had become the major
source of employment for social workers. But the squeeze on
public expenditure, the widening gap between needs and resources, the formal setting of priorities, all constituted external
pressures on practitioners. The hierarchical structures of departments, the inability to devote time to clients to undertake the kind
of social work practice taught on social work courses, the unresolved tension between the socially and politically committed
and those who saw their task as rendering individual small-scale
assistance, produced internal pressures within social work.

Casework in the sense of a therapeutic relationship stretching
over months and years was a luxury which the public sector was
unable to afford under the bombardment of referrals. But putting
a model of practice in its place proved difficult. Time-limited
intervention, contract theory, family therapy, systems theory and
the unitary approach, groupwork, behavioural modification,
patchwork, crisis theory all enjoyed their advocates as the litera-
ture of the 1970s and 1980s reflects; the diversity of approaches
used by social workers led on occasion to fierce doctrinal struggles.
The context in which these debates about relevant approaches were

conducted was one in which professionalism, in the sense of the autonomy of the individual practitioner, seemed ever more circumscribed by managerialism as procedural guidance and policy manuals buttressed a bureaucratic structure designed to minimise inconsistencies in practice.

Social work theory in Britain still reflects the twin influences of structured approaches to work with individuals and families, and of a neighbourhood-based practice drawing from Hadley and McGrath (1984). The former reflects the significance of agency influences in constructing relevant theory. Social work theory cannot exist in a vacuum divorced from the realities of practice. Those realities are of a large volume of referrals, many of them urgent, and a lack of staff to deal with them. Intervention has – by default – to be time-limited. If it is to withstand managerial scrutiny in the effective use of professional time, it has to be sharply focused on a specific task or tasks. If explicit objectives are to be achieved, the active participation of the client is required – and a formal contract can be a useful expression of shared priorities. The imposition of this structure can thus both serve as a rationing device in terms of worker-time and as a framework for practice.

Its relevance to those relationships which are by definition long-term, as with children in care or people with a sensory or intellectual handicap, is less obvious. The former group still tend to pass through the files of social work agencies with too little attention being paid to the importance of continuity of care. Most children leaving care will have had contact with over half-a-dozen social workers, and some in urban areas may have had many more. The care of mentally handicapped people was seen for many years as an appropriate task for unqualified staff but attitudes are changing with increased emphasis on building supports for carers.

Not all work can therefore be time-limited. But the other main current of development, neighbourhood work, has also been greatly influenced by agency setting. The dimension of the community was given insufficient attention in the press of new legislation, reorganisation and the explosion of referrals. The Barclay Report signalled its reemergence into the mainstream of practice but a number of teams had already adapted variants of the community social work model. The potential and some of the problems of developing neighbourhood work are discussed further in Chapter 2.

What is relevant to note here is that the rapidity of change in the external environment was mirrored by divergent views within social work, leaving the profession in a weak position to assert its unique contribution to politicians, the media or even to itself. The lack of confidence in the effectiveness of the personal social services was compounded by the hostile stance taken by central government to local government.

A Crisis in Central-Local Relationships

While the formal stance of successive Conservative administrations has been one of continuing support for welfare provision, there has been a shift in the ideology underlying policy. The original belief that the State is not the most efficient allocator of available resources has been extended to a passionate espousal of the virtues of the market. Under the banner of choice and competition, the concept of a deliberate enhancement of the plural system of welfare has developed in influence. It is intriguing to trace the strands of this development.

In 1979 the incoming Conservative Government signalled its attitude to local authority social services with proposed reductions in spending in the Public Expenditure White Paper which – had they been implemented – would have required closures and redundancies on a massive scale. The severe cuts sought did not materialise. Across the country, local authorities gave preferential treatment to social services in their decisions. Some of the reasons are evident. First, cutting services to vulnerable groups made little political appeal to local authorities regardless of political persuasion. Secondly, nearly half of all social services spending goes on residential services. Closing a home without available alternative accommodation is extremely difficult and runs counter to the development of community services as an alternative to hospital services. Thirdly, nearly half of social services spending goes on the elderly, a group of clients rapidly increasing in number. Again cuts to this group appeared politically and professionally impossible. As a result out-turn figures for 1980/1981 showed a growth of 2.7 per cent (3.3 per cent including joint finance) – a striking deviation from Government guidance.

There were, however, more serious tensions between central and local government than the failure to adhere to guidance on social services spending. Current expenditure on all services consistently outran public expenditure plans. Despite the much-publicised introduction of a Manpower Watch – a quarterly check on local government staffing numbers – the overall reduction in those employed was only 3 per cent in the first term of Conservative rule from 1979 to 1983. This contrasted with a 16 per cent reduction in the numbers of civil servants, although the latter figure owed more to the transfer of responsibilities to other parts of the public sector than to a real shedding of labour. Nevertheless it was used by politicians as a further indicator of the intractable nature of local government resistance to Government pressure.

The steady reduction in the share of local government expenditure financed by central Government grant led to steep rate rises in the early years of Conservative administration. Those years also saw the emergence of a new generation of local government leaders no longer willing to play the game of central–local relationships by the time-hallowed rules. Articulate, assertive and highly politicised leaders like Ken Livingstone, David Blunkett and Derek Hatton challenged the conventions and used the powers of local government to create a local state, an alternative source of funding and support for initiatives in tune with the political aspirations of the authority. Voluntary organisations and community groups had a crucial role to play in this alternative approach, creating new forms of citizen involvement through a focus on race and gender issues, particularly in London, and on the local authority as an instrument of economic regeneration.

The initial response from the Government to this challenge was financial. A new system of local government finance introduced in 1981/1982 calculated a local authority's entitlement to block grant by a complex formula to produce an assessment of its grant-related expenditure. The old joke was that only six people in the Department of the Environment fully understood the complexities of the Rate Support Grant. With the introduction of grant-related expenditure, that number was halved!

Any local authority wishing to spend substantially above the figure suggested by the Government for the aggregate of services in a local authority found its share of grant being reduced. With each year, the Government tightened the screw on recalcitrant local authorities through a complex system of targets and penalties. In 1982/1983 the basic system of ratecapping was introduced, which empowered central Government to set a maximum rate poundage for those authorities spending significantly more than their grant-related expenditure assessment.

The impact of ratecapping has been severe – if not quite as apocalyptic as suggested by political rhetoric. The creative accounting deployed by local authorities was able to defer the full rigour of the Government-imposed spending levels. By 1988 however, the inventiveness in circumventing the new controls had been exhausted and ratecapped authorities faced real reductions in spending of 10 per cent of more, with inescapable serious consequences for social services.

Linked to the abolition of the Greater London Council and other metropolitan authorities, ratecapping reasserted the primacy of central government in the struggle for influence. The struggle had soured attitudes and reinforced the determination of the Government to curtail the revenue-raising powers of local government. The device selected was the community charge introduced in Scotland in 1989 and in England and Wales in 1990.

The community charge has major implications for social policy both in its impact on taxation and its significance for future service growth. Rates were never popular as a means of raising revenue to cover local spending. Increasing more than the rate of inflation in many areas, unpredictable and subject to the political vagaries of the majority party, they were however broadly progressive, with those able to pay more – or at least those in that group who lived in large houses – paying the highest rates of local taxation. But they were unrelated to the use made of services by the household, with a single householder paying the same in rates as a family with several incomes and using local services extensively. Linking payment to usage has been the key principle adopted by the Government with each adult making an equal contribution to local spending.

The fundamental shift is one from an imperfect but broadly progressive form of taxation to one that is regressive. The poor working family are hardest hit as they are denied the modest protection afforded to those on social security. The effect will therefore be to worsen the poverty trap. The initial impact of the charge is likely to be a severe political constraint on raising the charge beyond the annual rate of inflation. This will be potentially serious for those services looking to increase their resources. Plans for any new developments are likely to be subject to close scrutiny. The financial thrust exemplified by the community charge is to squeeze local spending, and this has to be contrasted with the need for more extensive day domiciliary and residential services to support a community care strategy. This conflict is at the heart of the new role envisaged for personal social services.

A Changing Role for Personal Social Services

The extent of the shift in thinking about welfare which has come after a decade of Conservative rule may be seen in the open public and professional discussion of ideas previously considered fanciful. In that sense, the 1984 Buxton speech of the then Secretary of State for Social Services may have been ahead of its time. The lack of follow-up from the Department of Health and Social Security, despite repeated promises of a Green Paper, tended to dissipate the initial impact of the speech. In truth the speech was not wholly new or unexpected. Mrs Thatcher in one of her rare speeches on social issues had said, 'the volunteer movement is at the heart of all our social welfare provision. The statutory services can support the supporters and ease the pressure on volunteers with professional help and advice' (Thatcher 1981). Her first Secretary of State for Social Services, Patrick Jenkin, had similarly envisaged statutory services as 'a long stop for the very special needs going beyond the range of voluntary services' (Jenkin 1980).

Emphasis on the voluntary sector is not an exclusively Conservative phenomenon. As Labour Secretary of State, David Ennals launched the Good Neighbour campaign as an explicit recognition of the importance of neighbourly help in complementing and supplementing State services. What was distinctive about Mr Fowler's Buxton speech was that he went far beyond the ritualistic praise of the work of voluntary organisations, but began to sketch a model for delivering care which placed social services as a funding, enabling authority rather than one engaged in the direct provision of services.

The role envisaged by Mr Fowler had three key elements

defined as paramount responsibilities for each social services department. These were:

(a) a comprehensive strategic view of all available sources of care;
(b) a recognition that direct services were only part of the local pattern;
(c) a recognition that social services should promote and support the fullest possible participation of the other different sources of care that exist or which can be called into being.

There is nothing in those three elements which would be rejected by any Director of Social Services. What would be challenged is the assumption that there exists a vast untapped reservoir of potential care in the community, and that other forms of care are preferable to public provision which should become the provider of last resort.

The problems generated by an ideologically based preference for the private sector can be seen in the context of private residential care. By accident rather than design the Department of Health and Social Security has presided over an explosive growth in private provision. The extension of social security support to private and voluntary homes stimulated the rapid expansion of private care. Despite a national ceiling on the weekly charges supported by social security, the costs to the public purse have increased to over £1000 million – one-fifth of the total expenditure of social services on all client groups. Between 1979 and 1986, the number of elderly people in private and voluntary homes increased from 52 438 to 109 607 in England and Wales. There was no significant change in the number in local authority homes. From providing less than one-third of all places in 1979, the private and voluntary sector is now the dominant provider. It is a telling practical example of the shift in emphasis urged by Mr Fowler. That it was unplanned, unrelated to need, variable in quality and drew into residential care many who could have coped in the community with adequate support, is an equally telling comment on the deficiencies of the market.

The rapidity of the shift and the implications for public expenditure of this unplanned growth in residential care attracted the attention of the Audit Commission. It was trenchant in its criticism: 'At best there seems to be a shift from one pattern of residential care based on hospitals to an alternative support in many cases by Supplementary Benefits – missing out more flexible and more cost-effective forms of care altogether. At worst, the shortfall in services will grow with many vulnerable and disabled people left without care and at serious personal risk' (Audit Commission 1986, p. 2). It went on, after listing various options, to say 'The one option that is not tenable is to do nothing about present financial organisational and staffing arrangements' (p. 4).

The Griffiths Report was commissioned to review the need for change in the structure of community care. Rejecting structural change as premature and over-prescriptive, Griffiths set out a new approach to the management of community care. This placed local authorities in the primary role of designing, purchasing and organising community care. This would be funded through a specific Government grant subject to central government's approval of the local authority's proposals for the development of services. The emphasis throughout the Report was on the enabling role of social services rather than on their role as direct service provider. Choice and competition should be maximised by the further development of private services and the voluntary sector (Griffiths 1988)

The process of response to Griffiths will be a long one but the report struck a responsive chord among social services staff. What is evident from the summary of the past twenty years is the recurrence of certain themes, albeit in different guises – pressure on resources, political interest in informal care, and the strengthening of a plural system of welfare. The decade of Conservative rule has added two more – hostility to expanding public-sector bureaucracies, and an interest in applying market disciplines to welfare.

The professional response to these changing trends in social policy has been muted. Campaigns have been mounted against the reductions in public spending and their impact on clients. Some accommodation has been made to the interest in informal welfare through the renewed interest in community social work. Moves towards a market-orientation have evoked a less enthusiastic response. The Kent Community Care scheme used social workers in a brokerage role with a choice over the nature of provision in devising flexible packages of care. The scheme stands out as one of the few examples following the recommendation in the Barclay

Report favouring delegation of control over resources. Few social work teams have significant control over cash resources, although ironically practitioner decisions in relation to child care can involve the commitment of large-scale resources.

There has been a move back to greater specialisation in practice. After the headlong enthusiasm for generic practice in the wake of the reorganisation into social services departments, there has been a growing recognition that areas of practice benefit from the consolidation of expertise and specialist skills. Some of the specialisms have proved different from the clusters which existed prior to reorganisation – intake teams, welfare rights, child abuse; others like approved social workers can be related to the mental welfare officer of pre-Seebohm days. The specialisation has, however, been within the framework of a common training leading to the CQSW and a common organisational structure within which ninety per cent of social workers were located.

The trend to specialisation will continue to gather momentum. The approved social worker was given, under the Mental Health Act, responsibilities for which specialist training and expertise beyond that of other social workers was required. There is discussion of replicating that model particularly in the context of child care. A precedent exists in the appointment of guardians *ad litem* from the ranks of experienced and skilled practitioners.

The shifting organisational emphasis has now to reflect the greater entrepreneurialism demanded by both the Audit Commission and Griffiths. The entrepreneurial manager is still a rare sight in local government. Personnel policies, financial limitations, and public accountability lead to a deliberate pace of decision-taking and policy formation, designed to reduce risk and share responsibility. The ability of social workers to see all sides of a story is not the primary quality of successful entrepreneurs.

The strength of local government historically has lain in its ability to change and adapt. New financial and organisational structures for the delivery of community care will pose a major challenge. The requirement to promote a plural system of welfare challenges the deep-seated belief that only public-sector provision can secure consistency, quality and equity. If social services departments as at present constituted are unlikely to survive, what does that mean for social work itself? By looking at practice, training, organisation and management, some of the answers may begin to emerge.

2
Practice in Flux

Social work practice has changed dramatically in the years since the Second World War. As the Poor Law gave way to the legislative framework of the contemporary Welfare State, social workers shifted away from a role of administering welfare services to the poor, using social insurance and charities to secure adequate income levels for the poor. The postwar legislation stressed the wider responsibilities of promoting social welfare and led to the development of specialised casework services. The scale of need that was exposed by the reorganisation following the Kilbrandon and Seebohm Reports was such that the role of social workers was obliged to change once again. The direction and character of that change remain the subject of controversy.

In her study of social work between 1950 and 1975 Younghusband (1978) analyses the development of the postwar welfare services and the factors contributing to expansion. In a vivid phrase, she describes how 'curiosity burst free from its static or moralistic assumptions of an earlier period' (p. 25). As society grew more affluent in an age of full employment it equally became more willing to see and to respond to problems that had always been present but below the threshold of public and political awareness. The numbers of qualified social workers were still quite small before the Seebohm Report, and the expansion of the profession was an aspiration shared by politicians at both national and local level as well as by social workers themselves. They believed with an innocence and optimism now foreign to practice that more human individualised services responding to identified need would provide better social conditions for clients, and that social work itself, properly funded and supported, would bring about positive changes in the lives of clients. Their aim, reflected in the Seebohm recommendations, was to secure truly universal professional and personal social services to mirror the postwar achievements of universal free education and health care.

The Seebohm Report had as a major preoccupation the need to ensure that one social worker would deal with the problems of one family instead of the fragmentation by age group and problem category which prevailed at the time of the Report. But another important dimension to the Report was an explicit recognition of the importance of working with groups and communities as well as with individuals. 'Different divisions between methods of social work are as artificial as the difference between various forms of social casework . . . in his daily work the social worker needs all these methods to enable him to respond appropriately to social problems which involve individual, family, group and community aspects' (Seebohm 1968, p. 172).

The means whereby Seebohm envisaged that this integrated response to social need could be achieved was a single social worker dealing with all the social problems within the family. The label given was a 'generic social worker', although oddly the description appears nowhere in the Seebohm Report itself. There was widespread confusion and disorganisation in the early years of social services departments as practitioners were forced to grapple with social needs and legislative frameworks unfamiliar to them. The tension between the primacy of the community defined geographically with local workers offering a multi-purpose service, and the maintenance of specialist work as the basis for service delivery has dominated the years since Seebohm. Initially the fashion for genericism was dominant but even at its height the arguments for specialist models continued to be forcefully presented.

Specialisation

It is worth reflecting on the underlying reasons for specialisation. There are two key assumptions involved. First, the knowledge and range of skills required to deal adequately with the tasks required is too great for any individual practitioner. A better quality of service will therefore be obtained by focusing more narrowly on a defined group, and developing expertise in that specialised area of work. The second assumption is that not only will the quality of individual work be improved, but the organisational response to service delivery will also benefit by virtue of drawing together common needs and common service responses.

The nature of expertise has been helpfully analysed by Stevenson (1981, p. 48). She points out the problems peculiar to social work in the concept. First, there is within social work a suspicion of elitism and the claims by any group of practitioners to special skills or special status. Second, the current emphasis on partnership with clients and empowerment is difficult to reconcile with the possession by the social worker of exclusive knowledge. Neither objection is insuperable but they reflect important strands of thinking within the profession. The quest for expertise needs therefore to focus on what this actually means for clients, rather than on what it means for the practitioners. One area of concern has to be the ability of workers to keep abreast of developments. The proliferation of research findings and the dissemination of knowledge presents a formidable updating challenge for full-time academics. For practitioners it is an almost impossible task unless the focus is narrowed to a limited number of topics. Keeping abreast of current trends is therefore more feasible for those in a specialist role.

One of the recurrent criticisms of qualifying training for social work has been the lack of preparedness for the realities of practice of those coming from social work courses. In particular the absence of detailed knowledge of the legislative framework governing work with clients has been a source of continuing criticism. By concentrating staff in specialist teams, one not only narrows the range of knowledge required by the individual social worker but also creates potential reinforcement and cross-fertilisation. Workers derive greater confidence by building up experience rapidly. Clients too derive benefits from greater continuity of care and by contacts with a more limited number of social workers.

Since the initial moves to create a generic service there has been a slow but steady reversion towards greater organisational specialism. This can be traced through four strands of development – the impact of child-abuse inquiries, demographic changes, multi-disciplinary working and legislative pressure.

Child care

Reference has already been made to the knowledge explosion. In no area has this been more acute than in the highly sensitive and politicised area of child abuse. The sensitivity derives from the care required in handling complex family interactions while preserving a focus on the welfare of the children involved. The politicisation derives from the publicity inevitably accruing to child-abuse work, the scope it offers to critics of social work intervention, and its exposed position in relation to other disciplines and the courts. The spotlight of publicity shows no sign of abating and the issues raised by the Cleveland Inquiry (DHSS 1988) became material for debate in pubs and clubs as well as the House of Commons.

A common organisational response to pressure from elected members to demonstrate that 'there will be no Maria Colwell or no Cleveland here' – the favoured political rhetoric of some members – is to organise specialist teams with a high level of training, experience and support. The NSPCC does so through its network of Child Protection Teams. There are legitimate professional reasons for doing so as discussed above in a field of activity which is producing scores of research articles each month, which is stressful for practitioners, and which is time-consuming and high-risk for the organisation. The gains, however, have to be weighed against the potential problems arising from the fragmentation of child care work with child abuse, adoption and fostering, and intermediate treatment all having claims to separate organisational structures. Reproducing the overlap, duplication and muddled coordination described by Seebohm is a real danger. The development of specialisms in child-care work generally and child-abuse work specifically seems likely to continue because it satisfies professional and political aspirations.

Demography

Demography is not a word which figured large in social work's vocabulary when social services departments were being established. The Seebohm Report did identify the rapid increase expected in the numbers of persons over the age of 75, but not until the increase was actually being experienced by departments through the pressure of referrals did the full recognition of the problems of demographic change strike home. Some modest increment in Rate Support Grant negotiations has reflected the changing age structure of the population. Yet Parsloe and Stevenson found that social work students were uninterested in work with the elderly. Asked to identify preferences from nine client groups, social work students regarded only work with adult offenders as less attractive than work with the elderly (Parsloe and Stevenson 1978, p. 367).

The high status of child care and the pressures experienced in that area meant that social work resources were concentrated there with a consequent tendency for work with the elderly to be left to unqualified staff. Specialist teams were seen by some departments as a means of redressing this imbalance by ensuring the allocation of a number of qualified staff specifically to work with elderly and disabled people. Such teams also provided a vehicle for securing the full integration of occupational therapists.

Multidisciplinary work

The Court Report (1976) recommended the establishment in each health authority of a multidisciplinary team of professionals to be responsible for the assessment of children with special needs. At about the same time, the concept of community mental handicap teams was being developed and promoted as relevant to both children and adults (National Development Group 1977). Similar ideas have been promulgated in relation to community based services for elderly people, and those with a mental illness.

What these concepts have in common is a recognition that no single profession has a monopoly of skill, knowledge and expertise in dealing with the physical, social and psychological problems presented by these clients, that close coordination of inputs is desirable to achieve maximum impact, and that the establishment of a formal team is the best way of securing coordinated effort and the integration of different skills.

Multidisciplinary teams involve staff in crossing organisational boundaries. Where the worker has a specialist role, it is important that there is within the outposting organisation a clearly-established framework for support and consultation. This can often best be offered by a reference group of specialist staff. The impetus to multidisciplinary teams has therefore been paralleled by a move to specialist teams within social services.

Legislative framework

The Mental Health Act 1983 gave a major boost to specialisation by the inclusion in legislation of the concept of the approved social worker. This required those taking the social work decisions in situations where the liberty of the client was at issue to undertake special training and to demonstrate their competence and knowledge. The scale of the training was such that departments were obliged to identify workers to undertake this specialist function, and to weight their caseloads to ensure that there was an appropriate mix of mental health work to provide continuity of experience. A number of organisational models were developed to provide appropriate opportunities for the approved social worker, including deployment in specialist teams.

From time to time, the notion is canvassed of extending this concept of post-basic traning requirements to other specialist functions, in particular child abuse. While this has not yet been accorded legislative consideration, it could offer a potential model for training and practice building on the generic base of qualifying training.

The pattern of specialisation which has emerged is more differentiated and more developed than Seebohm envisaged yet the Report was remarkably prescient in recognising that 'as the service develops, specialisations will cluster differently and new types . . . emerge to meet new problems and needs and fresh conceptions of how these might be tackled' (Seebohm 1968, p. 162).

Community Social Work

There has been a powerful counteracting influence in the lobby for patch and community social work. Patch is nothing new, in the sense that social services delivery systems have to be based on geographical boundaries, whether of the local authority itself, a ward or group of electoral wards, or a neighbourhood clearly defined as distinctive. But the current enthusiasm for patchwork goes far beyond the concept of allocation by geography, which has long been in force, particularly in rural areas. Professor Hadley is the linking figure between the various expositions of patch. Writing with Hatch (Hadley and Hatch 1981), he linked the emergence of patch with a critique of the impersonal public sector bureaucracy. With McGrath, he developed a typology of indicators for locally-based social services (Hadley and McGrath 1980, 1984). In the Barclay report, Appendix A (written with Brown and White), he argued that the report's central recommendation of community social work – while welcome – did not go far enough in effecting fundamental changes in attitudes and practices (Barclay 1982).

Adopting Hadley's own list, one can identify the characteristics and preconditions of building services on this basis. The first and in some ways the most fundamental is size. The Seebohm concept of area offices assumed that these would serve a given population of 'between 50 000 and 100 000'. Hadley indicates a population of between 5000 and 10 000 as the appropriate basis for the patch. The role of the social worker is also changed from that of the individual delivering services through personal contact and intervention to one of the orchestration of community resources, using informal care, voluntary organisations and untrained patch-workers as the means of knitting together support systems for vulnerable individuals. With modifications, this concept was adopted in the Barclay report albeit with the somewhat forbidding label of social care planning.

To be effective in this role, Hadley suggests four requirements (Barclay 1982):

(a) the ability to locate and be accessible to local networks. This requires a pooling of knowledge about the strengths of the neighbourhood, and the development of good lines of communications.

(b) responsiveness and flexibility. In order to strengthen the informal care networks, services have to be flexible, sensitive and adaptable, responding to the need presented, rather than offering a set of services on a take-it-or-leave-it basis.

(c) developing additional resources. While not eschewing the need for more care resources funded from the public purse,

Hadley stresses the wider involvement of informal helpers, formal volunteers and voluntary organisations.

(d) understanding people and groups, and identifying with them. If this means anything, it is a gloss upon the accessibility to local networks referred to earlier.

Translating those requirements into a new pattern of community-orientated service delivery, Hadley identifies certain common organisational changes – localisation, integration, wider roles and greater autonomy. Of these the blurring of roles between the social worker and the patchworker ancillary is a major issue for practice. The lucid account which Currie and Parrott provide of the introduction of a community-orientated approach in an area team offers further indicators to the impact on practice of changing fieldwork roles. 'If . . . in a team approach, the unit of social work is seen as the team as a whole, rather than the individual, any rigid external definitions of what a worker can or cannot be permitted to do would be potentially very inhibiting' (Currie and Parrott 1986, p. 45).

They found unqualified social work assistants were able to make a major contribution to the work of the patch, supporting day care and residential provision, establishing groups for mentally handicapped adults, recruiting, selecting and training volunteers, and performing a range of tasks more frequently reserved for qualified staff. The Normanton study found a similar enhancement of the role played by unqualified and ancillary staff (Hadley and McGrath 1984).

Currie and Parrott are more sympathetic to the development of specialist skills than are the models developed by Hadley, which envisage a second tier of specialist workers to handle referrals from the primary social care team. For Currie and Parrott,

an analysis of any worker's workload would display a proportion which is:

1 random and undiscriminating (e.g. taken on in an emergency when on duty, or a just share of a particular type of case).

2 an identifiable and planned specialism within their caseload (e.g. prospective foster-parents, mentally handicapped children).

3 a substantial commitment by all workers, individually and jointly with others, to some liaison, group work, community work or volunteer initiative (Currie and Parrott 1986, p. 47).

The debate between community-centred models and specialist models has proceeded with vigour but has generated more heat than light. A major national study of practice is reported in the *British Journal of Social Work* (Challis and Ferlie 1987). Based on a study of just under 3000 fieldworkers, nearly 29% were found to be in formal specialist roles. Deployment of staff by client groups was the most favoured basis for practice (37%) followed by a patch approach (24%) and a generic basis (18%). When changes in process or contemplated were studied, the trend to specialist posts was more clearly emphasised, with significant shifts to formal specialisation. The study also confirmed the extent of informal specialisation, with 7 in every 10 area team social workers having over three-quarters of their caseload from one of the three main client groups – children and families, elderly and physically handicapped or mental health.

Hitherto the discussion has been based on the two major competing trends in practice development. Interestingly, both represent the influence of organisational structures on practice. While there may be strengths in diversity and in adopting the most relevant structures for the geographical area served, it would be unrealistic to accord too great a weight to rationality in decision-making.

The debate has assumed political overtones. The move to decentralise services has attracted interest and support from across the political spectrum. Stevenson comments quizzically, 'there are oddities in the political influences. . . , On the one hand, advocacy of the patch worker can be associated with the Left; its emphasis on the "humanisation" of the worker, the demystification of professionalism and the opportunity it gives for promoting cohesive social action fit well with this political stance. On the other hand . . . the right wing can espouse enthusiastically any system which promotes voluntary effort and the stimulation of caring networks' (Stevenson 1981, p. 66).

What is the Role of Social Work?

The debate within social work about the essential core of practice has taken place on a less emotional plane, although it reflects different value perspectives closely related to the debate about organisation.

Butrym (1976) built a practice model on the work of Halmos (1965), asserting the primacy of relationship in the helping process. She endorsed the fourfold summary of a helping relationship set out by Rogers (1953) as empathy, positive regard, genuineness and matched emotional response, and added a fifth borrowed from Halmos of commitment on the part of the counsellors. While these characteristics of the relationship are derived from psychotherapy. Butrym argues that the social work process, including both assessment and counselling, takes place in the context of a relationship. The relationship itself becomes a primary instrument for growth and development. Social workers are engaged with many people whose ability to function in society has been stunted by physical and emotional deprivations. By positive and purposeful use of the relationship, social workers can create a climate in which clients can develop in confidence, knowledge and functioning.

This is a traditional view of social work as casework, heavily influenced by writers from a psychotherapeutic perspective. While frequently criticised by writers as diverse as Wooton (1959) in her lambasting assault on the pretensions of social work, Sondheim in his brilliant lyric 'Gee, Officer Krupke' in West Side Story and Brewer and Lait (1980) from outside the profession, the view has also come under attack from social work colleagues Rees (1978), Goldberg (1979) and Sheldon (1986), who have all challenged the effectiveness of traditional methods of casework based on a supportive relationship.

An alternative model of practice proceeded from a different analysis of causation. The rediscovery of poverty by the Child Poverty Action Group focused attention on the structural influences on human behaviour – poverty, poor housing, and a stigmatising educational system. The response to social problems was seen as political and collective, utilising the power of the trade unions, and collective action to influence structural change. Simpkin (1983) and Corrigan and Leonard (1978) offer tentative glimpses of a model of practice which integrates that political perspective.

The psychodynamic and the overtly political model of practice stand at two ends of a broad spectrum of practice. Both have their adherents. The bulk of practitioners operate eclectically

somewhere in the middle, using attitudes and skills derived from
both, working sometimes as advocates, sometimes in community
network building and sometimes as counsellors in a helping
relationship. Those attempts to secure an integration of approach
are therefore of particular interest. The most important have been
the systems model developed by Pincus and Minahan (1973), and
the unitary approach favoured by Goldstein (1973).

The model developed by Pincus and Minahan is derived from
systems theory. It is based on four systems – the change-agent
system, the client system, the target system and the action system.
Strategies are discussed whereby the change agent working with
and through others can develop an action system to influence the
target system. While there may be a reaction against what sounds
rather mechanistic, the strength of the concept lies in its emphasis
on the interdependence of the various elements in the client's
social system. It does therefore integrate a concern for individual
needs and for change in the environment and community as of
equal significance in terms of potential impact on the client's
situation.

Goldstein also uses systems theory to develop a practice
methodology, which draws together elements of sociological and
psychological theory by looking at the interaction between social
worker and client as part of wider social systems. Therapeutic and
social action strategies can be regarded as differential strategies
rather than alternatives. The unitary model thus draws together
the strategy – evaluation, intervention and review – the target
(which may be the individual, family or network, or the community), and the sequential phases of induction, core and ending.

The strength of this integrated approach to practice may be seen
by reference to Currie and Parrott. The significance of their work
is its application of the theoretical model in an area team, using the
patch system to forge links with the community and the team itself
as the instrument of a flexible, responsive service tailored to
individual need. While not anchored in the theoretical model
applied by Currie and Parrott, the Barclay Report itself in its
espousal of community social work can be construed as seeking a
reconciliation of the social care planning role and individual work.
'Understanding the internal worlds of individuals and families will
remain important but increasing attention will need to be given to
theories which help to explain the interaction of individuals in

groups, localities, organisations and communities.' (Barclay, p. 209)

What Theories are Used by Practitioners

Three elements have come together to exercise a powerful influence on practice. The work of Reid and Shyne (1969) directed attention to the beneficial results of time-limited and focused intervention. In collaboration with Epstein, Reid (1972) established the benefits of a contractual approach to practice. 'Use of contracts helps to avoid certain perennial problems in social work practice: misunderstandings between worker and client as to the former's intentions and the latter's difficulty; lack of clarity on the part of both as to what they are to do together; drift and scatter in the focus of treatment' (Reid and Epstein 1972). The move towards greater openness in relation to sharing records with clients has helped to direct attention to explicit statements of objectives for the work being undertaken. In combination the three factors constitute a sharper, tighter approach.

Assessment has emerged as a core skill. The volume of work coming to social work agencies has afforded plentiful opportunity for practice. Drawing on Vickery's assessment model (1977), Coulshed suggests five questions:

1 what are the problems in this situation?
2 who are the clients?
3 what are the goals?
4 who has to be changed or influenced?
5 what are the tasks and roles of the social worker:

These questions have to be answered at the level of the individual, the group, the neighbourhood, the organisation and the wider environment (Coulshed 1988, p. 19).

While counselling remains the primary means of intervention, using the word as the Barclay Committee did to describe the range of supportive, problem-solving, developmental and crisis interviewing, it has been buttressed by enhanced understanding of human behaviour. Crisis theory provides a framework for understanding and working positively with people in a crisis situation. Family therapy offers insights and working methods for use in complex family interactions. Groupwork offers opportunities for sharing experiences of learning and growth in a way which can produce dramatic gains. And behavioural social work is growing in influence as workers gain confidence in using structured and systematic techniques of intervention.

The advocacy role has become ever more important with the growing complexity of social security and housing benefit systems and the progressive dismantling of hard-won rights and entitlements for claimants.

With the interest in work with community networks and empowering groups and communities, social work practice is thus vibrant and ever-developing. Its eclecticism is both its strength and its weakness. Its strength is in facilitating an appropriate range of responses to problems presented (the relevance of crisis theory to effective work with victims of disasters like the Bradford fire or the *Herald of Free Enterprise* is an illustration). Its weakness is that its apparent lack of coherence and its variety makes it difficult for those outside social work to understand what social workers are doing and why.

Who Does Social Work?

While this attempt to reconcile different approaches to practice has continued, another strand has been the elusiveness of attempts to define the social work task. A BASW working party report of that title was comprehensively criticised, more because of the definition it proferred than its content, which stands up well to rereading. It suggested that 'social work is the purposeful and ethical application of personal skills in interpersonal relationships directed towards enhancing the personal and social functioning of an individual, family, group or neighbourhood, which necessarily involves using evidence obtained from practice to help create a social environment conducive to the well-being of all' (BASW 1977, p. 19). It is interesting to examine that definition in the light of the preceding discussion about competing claimants for the soul of social work. The first clause represents the traditional counselling role espoused by Butrym. The second represents a nod

towards family work, group work and community work as equally
valid methods of intervention, and the last clause was added to
satisfy the advocates of social action.

An important element in the discussion of the social work task
was the attempt to differentiate the social work role from that
appropriately carried out by other fieldwork staff. This has been a
recurrent issue in social services departments, compounded by the
scale of the enterprise and the diversity of tasks undertaken. When
less than one in seven of the staff employed are social workers, the
tendency to equate social work with social services (not wholly
absent from this book) arouses both confusion and resentment on
the part of those who are not social workers. The bombardment of
referrals put pressure on departments to devise ways of coping
using other fieldwork staff. Two pieces of evidence suggest that the
demarcation lines were never drawn clearly.

Parsloe and Stevenson found that the differentiation between
social workers and social work assistants was less evident in
relation to the tasks performed than it was in relation to the client
groups served, with social work assistants frequently carrying a
caseload of elderly and handicapped clients.

> Several related but separate factors seem to explain the pattern
> of work – they include the perceived needs of the range of
> clients served by social services departments in terms of the
> service provided and the appropriate level of staff to undertake
> the work; and the assistants' job satisfaction and the dominance
> of the case as the unit of work which affected attitudes about
> 'sharing' work between different grades of staff (Parsloe and
> Stevenson 1978, p. 141).

Of particular significance here are the twin assumptions that
work with the elderly is more practical and straightforward than
with other client groups, and that social work skills in using
relationships were more applicable to work with children and
families which necessitated a higher level of sensitivity and knowledge. Despite the bid to redress the balance through specialist
teams, there remains a significant disparity between social work
time available to children and families and that available for all the
other client groups put together.

The BASW report sought to provide a conceptual framework to

distinguish the different types of knowledge and skill required, and
concluded that the assessment process was of central importance.
It outlined three criteria for work allocation:

(a) *Level of client vulnerability* This covered physical, psychological and social vulnerability. Not all acute physical needs dictate
a qualified social worker, but the report suggested that if the work
required involves using personal skills in interpersonal relationships to enhance social functioning, it should be a social work task.

(b) *Degree of complexity* This suggested that the number of
factors in the client's social situation, the degree of change needed,
and the degree of use of one's own personality required from the
worker were relevant factors in determining whether the need was
for a qualified social worker.

(c) *The significance of decision-making* Here it is suggested that
loss of liberty through care proceedings, mental health admissions
or prison sentences should be contingent only on the involvement
of social workers (a view implicitly endorsed in the 1983 Mental
Health Act). It extended this view to planned changes of
residence, or significant changes in legal status, e.g. adoption,
guardianship, and so on.

While undoubtedly useful as descriptions of the factors which
actually influence allocation, the framework does not greatly assist
workload allocation following initial referral, for the answer to the
three issues raised would only be known following an assessment.
The large numbers of elderly people referred to departments
usually for relatively straightforward help make it impossible to
contemplate full initial assessments of all referrals being made by
social workers. If a differentiated model is to be sustained, a way
has to be found of using routine assessment reports to identify
cases requiring social work skills and allocate accordingly.

What Role has Social Work?

There is an unresolved issue about the role fulfilled by social
workers in contemporary society. Butrym (1976), Corrigan and
Leonard (1978) and Davies (1981) proceeding from different
positions would reach the same conclusions that social work exists

and is publicly funded in order to uphold prevailing social norms. In Davies' words, 'the essence of social work is maintenance: maintaining a stable, though not a static society, and maintaining the rights of and opportunities for those who in an unplanned, uncontrolled community would go to the wall' (Davies 1981, p. 209). Corrigan and Leonard challenge the legitimacy of those class-based norms and argue for a practice that recognises the importance of using working-class strengths and building collective solutions to social needs rather than working from an individual-istic perspective.

Jordan (1984, 1987) challenges the concept of maintenance, at least in the way in which it is presented by Davies. He contends that the peculiar contribution of social work is its readiness to forsake formal roles and to use informal methods of negotiation, which recognise the importance of how people perceive their own needs and how informal social systems work. Patchwork, with its emphasis on low-key, locally negotiated solutions and its positive use of informal networks, is more conducive to this approach than is an explicit commitment to the essential maintenance role of social work.

Breaking Down the Barriers

The boundary between residential work and fieldwork repays examination, for greater readiness to span this divide is one of the characteristics of the changing pattern of services. Younghusband acknowledges, 'there was little interest in the residential task in the care or control of adults during the 1950's and 1960's' (Young-husband 1978, Vol. 2, p. 182). With the advent of the Central Council for Education and Training in Social Work, special options for residential workers were developed on social work courses, and the advent of CSS in 1977 provided another vehicle for qualifying training. Progress in increasing the overall propor-tion of qualified staff has been very slow. Twenty years after the Williams Report, which found over 80 per cent of the full-time care staff had no qualification other than experience, a CCETSW report suggested that 68 per cent of residential staff were in the same position (CCETSW 1987).

The imbalance between fieldwork and residential training levels has been a source of status differential with residential workers justifiably regarding themselves as disadvantaged in pay and status compared with fieldwork colleagues. The functional separation of management of residential and day care resources from that of fieldwork further widened the sense of separateness. The Personal Social Services Council, in its short existence, made an important contribution to the development of residential care. *Living and Working in Residential Homes* (PSSC 1975) defined residential care as 'the produce of two different responses to social problems; the creation of group living to meet people's needs for suitable accommodation and possibly their social and emotional needs; and the provision of care'. The PSSC said squarely that physical care was not enough, and that the residential social work task was to maintain choice and personal independence for residents, maximising their participation in decision-making. As a statement of aspiration, this 'horticultural' model of personal growth and development as the primary task for residential work is now widely accepted in theory. Practice still falls far short.

The Barclay Report listed eight problems in shifting residential care into the mainstream of social work thinking. These were:

1 *Stigma* The legacy of the Poor Law, the sociological work of Goffman and others on institutions, and societal assumptions about personal failure or inadequacy on the part of residents combine to create a stigma attaching to residential care.

2 *Segregation* The separation into client groups which characterises residential care means that residents often lose contact with the wider community and with other social groups, living in settings where the scope for forming relationships is inherently limited.

3 *Dominance of fieldwork assumptions* The central importance of tending and nurturing in residential care tends to be subordinate to fieldworkers' preoccupation with treatment and change.

4 *Bureaucratic influences* The hierarchical structures of public sector bureaucracies inhibit a flexible spontaneous response to needs. From order books for children's clothing to large institutional kitchens, the requirements of administration – sometimes legitimate in terms of costs – militate against a truly personal residential care service.

5 *Delayed admissions to residential care* The emphasis on

supporting individuals at home means that by the time of admission, 'residential staff are sometimes given impossible tasks – like seeking to develop caring relationships with a group of resentful teenage offenders; or creating life and sharing among senile elderly people' (Barclay 1982, p. 57).

6 *Assumptions about the superiority of family life* Fieldworkers rated family life, however flawed or destructive, more highly than institutional life – a view challenged by many residents.

7 *Poor conditions of service* These led to rapid turnover, and a drift of qualified staff to fieldwork settings.

8 *The numbers of untrained staff* The dearth of progress in this area was discussed above.

These obstacles can be described as organisational, relating to the bureaucracy and its terms and conditions; as sociological in terms of stigma and segregation; and as psychological where the values and assumptions of fieldwork serve to compound divisions between fieldwork and residential care. The first two groups may be intractable, but there are ways of bridging the interface between field and residential work.

Keyworker is a phrase which is frequently bandied about but not always with the clarity that one would wish. Developed in a general statement between BASW and RCA (1976), the concept gives responsibility for carrying out the agreed plan in relation to a client to one designated worker. The task of the worker, who may come from either field or residential settings, is to see that the plan is carried through by the parties involved. The task is frequently confused with that of the primary worker, who has most day-to-day contact with the resident. Sometimes the two roles may be carried by one person, but this will depend on the amount of work in the wider environment.

Splitting the two roles can be cumbersome. There has been increasing interest in the one worker carrying both fieldwork and residential responsibilities for the resident. In the context of residential child care, this involves the residential worker taking an active role in assessing the strengths of the family situation pending return home or taking responsibility for placement with foster parents. For the child in care, the proliferation of significant adults can be confusing. The continuity and stability which this merger of key and primary worker can bring is therefore a major advantage. For the mentally handicapped person moving from life in a hostel to more independent living in the community, the support of familiar staff is critical and where one worker can take responsibility for the preparation, resettlement and subsequent support, confidence can be built up gradually.

This concept was endorsed by the Wagner Committee which laid great emphasis on the importance of continuity for residents both in terms of consistency from staff and the maintenance of links with a resident's former life. In addition, the Committee identified four other principles as the basis for good practice in residential care:

Caring – this should be personal, and residents should feel valued, safe and secure;

Choice – each resident's right to exercise choice over their daily life should be respected;

Change – for residents, the opportunity for continued development; for staff, a commitment to respond to changing needs;

Common values – ensuring that practice is based on a shared philosophy and values (Wagner 1988, p. 60).

As a reflection of this deliberate bridging of the traditional boundaries as they affect staff in residential settings, a rethink is underway about the traditional pattern of residential provision. Homes for the elderly are being questioned as a result of the explosive growth of private residential care, and the possibility of other approaches more aligned with the attitudes to indépendence, individuality and choice espoused by social services is being explored. The forty-place home is unlikely to survive in the face of joint developments with housing associations offering greater privacy, greater space and greater flexibility for residents. Instead of a standard package of care, residents could be offered a flexible range of services dependent on their need. Nursing units could be located on site so that lifetime care could be offered. The private sector is already moving in this direction, providing guarantees to elderly people that they will remain within the development unless there is a need for hospital care.

Two elements can be identified in the best of new developments. These are normalisation – an ugly word but essentially asserting the importance of maintaining as normal a lifestyle as is feasible

– and domestic-scale provision. Schumacher's dictum that 'small is beautiful' can be as relevant to elderly people as to other care groups. Resource centres with some limited residential or respite provision are one way in which future services may seek to address a range of needs. They would offer day care, night sitting services, specialist advice and assessment as well as residential and respite care. They would be the natural base for specialist social workers and could be a vehicle to break down the barriers of the segregated residential unit to draw in the community as part of a process of mutual help.

These approaches are reflected in the Wagner Report, which stresses the need to make residential care a positive choice and not something which happens by default. Residential care needs to be part of a spectrum of care based on the needs of individual clients, and reflecting, in the words of the Association of Directors of Social Services' evidence to the Committee, the concepts 'that small is beautiful, that local is best and that normalisation is the aim'. (Wagner 1988, p. 161)

The Future

The turbulent political and professional environment in which social work has operated means that social work practice has often been reactive. At times the gap between theory and practice has been too wide, especially in departments suffering bombardment – a widely-used term describing the pressure of a rising tide of referrals. Yet there has been a major development of the knowledge base of social work practice, with social workers recognising that no single approach is appropriate for all clients.

In the light of the divergent influences on practice and the differing value systems of practitioners, any generalisations about future trends must of necessity be tentative. But some strands are sufficiently consistent to provide a basis for judgement.

First, there will be no unequivocal resolution of the specialist–generalist debate, although current trends in favour of a greater degree of specialisation reported by Challis and Ferlie (1987) are likely to be accentuated. Secondly, the moves to break down the rigid boundaries between fieldwork, day care and residential work will gather momentum with the rising costs of residential care, the advent of a unified training, and a steady if undramatic increase in qualified staff willing to work across traditional demarcation lines. Thirdly, the area office will cease to be the focal point of service delivery with the development of resource centres offering alternative venues for specialist teams, and with moves to outposting of workers as a means of strengthening linkages with neighbourhoods and communities. Fourthly, the broader view of social work reflected in qualifying training will encompass much of the work, particularly with elderly and handicapped people, now being carried by social work assistants and ancillary staff, leading to a redefinition of the service role appropriate for untrained fieldwork staff. Fifthly, there will be increased emphasis on locality planning jointly with health for neighbourhoods and communities.

Locality planning as operated in the health service draws together professional staff and community leaders active in a given geographical area to identify deficits in existing service provision, to improve coordination of professional effort and shape the future planning of services (King and Court 1984). Bridging the gap between the professional service planner and the recipients of services has mutual benefits in heightening the responsiveness of plans to local needs, and in strengthening the local awareness of problems and priorities.

Most of these themes have been developed previously, but the scope for moving away from the Seebohm model of the area office as the hub of service delivery justifies further examination. The Seebohm Report was in reality far more flexible in its concept of the area office than has been seen in application.

> Experiments in associating area offices with other locally based services should be encouraged: health centres, primary schools, libraries, children's playgrounds, day nurseries or even coffee shops . . . are all possibilities (Seebohm 1968, p. 1983).

Few of these experiments have come to pass. Fifteen years later, the Barclay Report suggested three ways of moving out from area offices: locally-based patch teams, resource centres and attachment. The outposting envisaged was health centres and schools although other bases could be considered – social security offices, factories, office blocks are all possibilities if a real commitment could be developed to an outposting model. Such a radical rethink of the location of social workers may be needed once the area office model begins to fragment, if the service offered is to be responsive to community needs.

The Griffiths Report (1988) contains ideas which could give a substantial push to new settings for the organisation of practice. The suggestion that companies may in future years come to view meeting the community care needs of their former employees in much the same way as the provision of an adequate pension scheme, an integral part of the package of conditions offered by the firm, is a visionary concept. Industry-based social work has never taken root in Britain in contrast to other parts of Western Europe, but it could if companies responded to the Griffiths challenge. The growth in the private and voluntary sector of provision implicit in Griffiths' proposals offers a range of alternative settings as service-giving agencies move into fields previously reserved for local authorities as monopoly providers.

The recommendation in the Griffiths Report that local authorities should coordinate the inputs from a range of agencies, to develop individually-tailored packages of care, will inevitably focus attention again on the thorny issue of how that coordination can best be achieved in practice. Developing services which are closer to the user offers the prospect of linking with community networks and ensuring the full use of informal resources available in the locality. The issue for local government is how far that process can be reconciled with representative democracy. Are service-users to be involved as advisers through consumer forums or Barclay's stillborn child, local welfare advisory committees, or are they to be given real control over resources and how they are distributed? The rhetoric of decentralisation sometimes appears to imply a transfer of power from elected members to unaccountable neighbourhood groups. T. Kubisa (quoted in Murray 1987), an advocate of decentralisation, recognised this and argued, 'it is naive to argue that the political process can be usurped by other processes' and pointed out that those who are not current users also have a right to a say in the shape of service provision.

Practice then is still wrestling with how best to achieve the aspiration of the Seebohm Report to involve clients and community in the planning process. The development of the market in welfare provision means that clients as consumers have at least

some influence on the shape and pattern of services, for they can
choose whether or not to place a monetary value on the service.
The deficiencies of this monetarisation of choice are discussed in
Chapter 8.

3

Unchanging Values?

In this book, the word 'profession' has sometimes been used to describe the occupational group known as social workers. It has been used to convey a sense of shared attitudes and values common to that occupational group. Its use reflects the writer's belief that there is a broad consensus justifying this use of the word, but it has to be conceded that this belief is by no means universally shared. The justification for use of the word in its narrower sense as a clearly-defined, self-regulating group with its own code of ethics is even more open to challenge, for the debate about the legitimacy of social work as a profession has been a recurrent theme over the past forty years.

In this chapter, the argument will be advanced that there is a recognisable core set of values which characterises social work, but that the continuing validity of those values has been under challenge particularly in the last decade. That challenge has come from the organisational context of social work, from the emergence of new preoccupations which bring some social work values into conflict with others, and from a radical critique of traditional values as paternalism disguised as professionalism. Social workers tend to shy away from thinking about value questions. They are not easy and the nature of practice is such that feel and instinct are more influential in shaping responses to situations than a thoughtful philosophical analysis. Yet virtually every aspect of practice raises difficult issues of rights – the rights of the child set against the rights of the parents, the rights of the individual against the rights of neighbours and society, and the rights of the social worker to seek to influence the client's own wishes and preferences.

What is a Profession?

A profession is characterised by a distinctive body of knowledge and skill shared by its members. A more cynical view is that professions are those occupational groups which have achieved a situation of high status or power, supporting Shaw's dictum that professions are conspiracies against the laity. In its evidence to the Barclay Committee, NALGO was unequivocal in its view that there was no generally recognised body of skill and knowledge which distinguished social work from other occupations. Testing that view is therefore a useful starting point for an examination of social work.

The clearest formulation of the knowledge base required for practice is supplied by Bartlett (1970):

1 Human development and behaviour, and the reciprocal influences of man and the total environment.
2 Psychology with particular reference to the psychology of giving help.
3 Communication, and how words, gestures and activities convey messages.
4 Group process, and the reciprocal relationships between the individual and the groups.
5 The impact of culture, including religious beliefs, law, values and other social institutions on individuals, groups and communities.
6 Relationships between individuals, and between individuals and groups.
7 The community, its processes, development, resources and needs.
8 The structure, organisation and methods of social services.
9 The self-awareness to acknowledge the impact of individual feelings and attitudes on professional functioning.

Few would argue that this knowledge base is exclusive to social work. It comprises elements derived from psychology, sociology, anthropology and psychiatry, yet despite its mixed origins it does constitute a recognisable and distinctive core. The Barclay Report described the core knowledge as 'practical information for immediate use, and knowledge that provides insight into the behaviour of people, organisations and societies, and into how that behaviour is likely to change under the influence of alternative courses of action' (Barclay 1982, p. 152).

Translating that knowledge into skills is the task of practice teaching. The skills required of a social worker can be identified in three clusters. First, there are skills in establishing and using relationships. Relationships are still at the heart of social work practice. Regardless of the task and regardless of the setting, social workers have to be able to make relationships with clients, colleagues and with others in the community. That requires skills in listening to others, skills in being able to show respect for the other, however one may feel about previous behaviours, skills in communication, and skills in being able to use personal qualities of warmth and concern in the context of an involuntary relationship. While some referrals come direct from the client, the majority reflect concern expressed by relatives or other community figures like general practitioners, councillors or voluntary workers.

Secondly, there are skills in assessment, analysis and evaluation. Relationships can be therapeutic. The benefits to individual clients of knowing that one person in their world cares, can be trusted and can tolerate their anger and frustration should never be underestimated. But social work is more than therapy, and the social worker has to work in an organisational framework which sets out certain obligations to be fulfilled in terms of record-keeping, case planning and review. Skills in handling information, analysing the factors impacting on the problem situation, and developing a workable plan of action are all key components.

Thirdly, there are operational skills in carrying through plans effectively. Skills in negotiation, in collaboration, in advocacy and in 'networking' are all important in translating a plan into reality. Assessment, analysis and evaluation can be wholly cerebral activities but making things happen is a practical skill.

These three clusters identified in the Barclay Report, when allied to the knowledge base discussed above, are distinctively those of social work, although each has overlapping elements with other disciplines. NALGO's contention, therefore, is open to serious doubt, and one wonders whether it reflects an anti-professional feeling within the union rather than an objective view of the current state of the knowledge base of social work. But if the beginnings of core knowledge can be discerned, the claims of social work to full professional status can be challenged on other grounds. Whilst having a Code of Ethics, the social work profession controls neither the use of the term 'social worker' nor training and entry to the profession. The reorganisation of training, and the reawakening of debate about a General Social Work Council, may offer opportunities to consolidate greater recognition for social work. Assumptions about the desirability of such a move rest on the basis of shared values within the profession. The nature of these values and the degree of their universal acceptance is discussed below.

Ethics and the Social Worker

The International Federation of Social Workers – a grouping of over 40 national associations of social workers drawn from every continent – adopted an International Code of Ethics in 1976. It sets out five major principles:

1 Every human being has a unique value.
2 Every individual has the right to self-fulfilment.
3 Each society . . . should function to provide the maximum benefits for all of its members.
4 The professional social worker has the objective to devote objective and disciplined knowledge.
5 The professional social worker has a primary obligation to the objective of service.

Couched in the opaque and general language of international organisations, these principles nevertheless contain some important statements adjudged to be of worldwide relevance. They assert the individual worth of every citizen but also the obligation on society to create the conditions for the self-fulfilment of individuals. On the social worker are laid the obligations of service to the individual and to the community, and the promotion of disciplined knowledge.

In these statements one may trace what Merton termed the threefold elements of social values in the concept of profession:

first, the value placed on systematic knowledge and the intellect: knowing. Second, the value placed upon technical skill and trained capacity: doing. Third, the value placed upon putting this conjoint knowledge and skill to work in the service of others: helping (Merton 1968).

The BASW Code of Ethics also reflects that trinity in its assertion that

> social work has developed methods of practice which rely on a growing body of systematic knowledge and experience. . . , He (the social worker) acknowledges a professional obligation, not only to increase his personal knowledge and skill but also to contribute to the total body of professional knowledge (BASW 1975).

This explicit statement of the knowledge base of social work is accompanied by a clear commitment to continuing professional education and training to enhance the capacity of the worker. And the Principles of Practice published with the Code set out the helping responsibility for the client in more personal and concrete terms.

Essentially codes of ethics can do no more than establish general guidelines. The nature of social work does not readily lend itself to specific prescriptions for conduct. The rights of the client are not unfettered, and will frequently bring conflict with the rights of others. The Cleveland child-abuse inquiry raised important issues of the primacy of the rights of children to protection from abuse and exploitation compared with the rights of parents to a family life free from well-meaning but officious and destructive intervention. Social workers are all too familiar with balancing rights and responsibilities in this way. What is important is to test whether the general guidelines set out in the Code of Ethics command widespread acceptance.

While the Code of Ethics was challenged by a minority of BASW members at the 1975 Annual General Meeting as conservative and elitist (the fashionable boo-words of the time) it has not been subject to sustained criticism from within the main body of social work. There are two possible explanations for this apparent acceptance. First, the Code – while designed to be adapted and amended in the light of changing social needs – adequately captures the general guidelines sought by social workers. The second and less flattering explanation is that the Code – which is binding only on members of BASW and thus on a minority – is regarded as an irrelevance not worth serious debate and challenge. There is some truth in both explanations. That group of social workers active within BASW may be assumed to be those most likely to be concerned with the development of professional status, yet they have not sought to make any major alterations to the 1975 version of the Code. The minor changes made reflect the increased emphasis on clear statements against racism and discrimination on grounds of sexual orientation. Many social workers would reject instinctively a Code of Ethics as carrying too many connotations of the traditional and exclusive professions, distanced by power and status from those they purport to serve.

There is a deep-seated anti-professionalism within social work, which sometimes leads its adherents into murky areas of self-contradiction, as in NALGO's submission to the Barclay Committee. If social work has no distinctive skills and knowledge, and professional training is a distancing process of socialisation into the so-called profession, the case advanced by NALGO for greater recognition of the difficulties facing social workers, and higher remuneration, look decidedly flimsy. While there is no consensus within social work about professionalism, there is more common ground than might initially be supposed from the position set out by the union in its evidence.

First, social work's aspirations to professionalism cannot be based on emulating medicine, the law and accountancy. None of those who advocate a model of professional self-regulation would regard the older professions as offering an acceptable model. Secondly, any model for social work has to be seen as serving client interests directly rather than professional self-interest. Thirdly, the values underlying the Code of Ethics would be widely supported within social work. The dissentients would be those following a Marxist analysis, who would see the emphasis in the Code on individual autonomy and self-realisation as the expression of 'the dominant ideologies necessary to the reproduction of the relations of production. These ideologies are expressed in

terms of the cult of individualism and in psychology in an endeavour to seek for basic human personality not properly related
to the social circumstances under which humans live' (Corrigan
and Leonard 1978, p. 122). From this viewpoint, the Code of
Ethics would itself be a limited and constricted view of the
dilemmas facing social workers, distorted by the individualistic
orientation of the Code.

Without entering into the sterile debate of whether social work
is a profession, a semi-profession or an occupation with professional aspirations, it may be more helpful at this stage to
concentrate on the process in which social workers engage. First,
there is a strong service orientation throughout social work with a
shared desire to give one's best to the recipients of the service.
Secondly, there is a functional role accorded to social work in
mediating between society's needs and the rights of vulnerable
individuals. Thirdly, social workers in discharging that role are
expected by society to display skill, knowledge and commitment
going beyond that of a local government functionary. The values
which underpin the service orientation may be shared by most
social workers but they are rarely analysed. That analysis is
important if the challenge of Corrigan and Leonard is to be
met.

Three Types of Values

Levy (1973) offers a helpful grouping of social work values into
three categories: values as preferred conceptions of people, values
as preferred outcomes for people, and values as preferred instru-
mentalities for dealing with people.

Conceptions of people

The emphasis on individualism discussed above is paramount
here. Each individual is regarded as having inherent worth regardless of actual achievements or behaviour. A psychopathic
rapist and an aggressive dementing elderly client are both
accorded respect as a person. Linked to this view is a belief in the
human capacity for change, development and greater fulfilment.

Blom-Cooper (Beckford 1985) writes scathingly of the social worker's rule of optimism, but the resilience which social workers display in the face of apparently intractable difficulties owes much to the view of human nature underpinning social work practice. The relationship between the individual and society is the central purpose of social work intervention, and a recognition that individual fulfilment is dependent upon others is an important value-statement of the social nature of man.

Outcomes for people

This group of values deals with society's obligations for the wellbeing of its citizens. These include the provision of opportunities for growth and development, freedom from hunger, inadequate education, discrimination and stunted life-chances. Social work does not have an exclusive concern with the improvement of social functioning, but its stance derives from the impact of deprivation on the weak and vulnerable.

Dealing with people

This group of values is most clearly reflected in codes of ethics. The preferred conceptions of people and outcomes for them are reflected in the ways in which social workers are obliged to deal with clients. Certain standards of behaviour are implicit in the social work role whether or not the worker specifically accepts a professional code. These include the respect for confidentiality, the precedence of professional responsibility over personal interests and a conscious attempt to widen the range of choice and decision-making powers available to social work's clients.

The acceptability of these three clusters has now to be tested against some of the pressures and challenges which have emerged in the post-Seebohm era. The implications of large-scale public-sector bureaucracies as a base for professional values are considered together with issues presented by newly emergent preoccupations like child sexual abuse. Racism and sexism are specifically addressed in some professional codes but some anti-racist strategies raise important ethical issues. Radical social workers remain deeply suspicious of talk of values, and the degree to which their practice expresses different value-positions is an important area for examination.

Organisational Pressures

Social work values have underpinned the development of social services although social workers are less than one-seventh of the workforce. The explosive growth of the early seventies saw an increase in functions and responsibilities, and a consequent increase in the number of management tiers interposed between social workers and the Director of Social Services. The complexity of organisational relationships, and the pressure arising from child abuse, led departments into an emphasis on procedures. The limits imposed by departments do control practitioner-discretion, but this is not peculiar to social work. 'Discretion like the hole in the doughnut does not exist except as an area left open by a surrounding belt of restriction' was the vivid phrase coined by Dworkin (1977, p. 52) to describe the nature of discretion in a bureaucracy. The impact of managerialism has been to tighten that belt of restriction and to limit the freedom of manouvre of the individual worker.

That tightening of restriction affects the ability of the worker to put into action some of the value systems discussed above. It is conditioned by resource constraints and by prescribed limitations on individual decision-making. As employees, social workers have to operate in agencies where difficult decisions about priorities have to be made. This is one of the areas identified by Rhodes (1986) as ways in which bureaucracies undermine both professional and personal concepts of morality. First, the obligations of the worker to client and to professional code are subordinated to organisational requirements which even subvert personal morality. Thus a vagrant would expect fifty pence or a pound towards a sandwich and cup of tea from a compassionate, socially concerned individual. But when that individual is a duty officer in a busy inner-city office, the response to the vagrant will be dictated

by organisational norms rather than individual views about inequalities in the distribution of wealth.

Secondly, social relations are defined impersonally by the categorisation of clients with an appropriate response in terms of
frequency of contact or pattern of service being determined by
reference to client category. By depersonalising the worker–client
contact, the social distance between the two is reinforced.

Thirdly, the development of specialisation leads to a distancing effect from ordinary moral responses. Whether it is with
child sexual abuse or profound disability or senile dementia,
the frequency of exposure to acute problems tends to blunt
sensibilities.

Fourthly, the impact of hierarchies with some decisions explicitly
removed from frontline workers adds to the sense of distance
between worker and client, for the worker does not have exclusive
and personal responsibility.

Translating these influences to the value-sets discussed above,
one can see that they do limit the ability of the worker to respond
to his fullest ability in meeting client need. The categorisation of
clients, and specifically the priority ranking which frequently
accompanies categorisation, impairs the response to individual
need. The scarcity of resources means that the worker's role will
often be that of the rationing agent delivering services which the
worker knows are inadequate to meet the needs presented. When
political decisions are taken by the employing authority which
impose hardship through increased charges or curtailed services,
the social worker can be drawn into making decisions about which
clients have the greatest need. There is nothing inherently wrong
with rationing when this is done with integrity and fairness, but
when the rationing process actually impairs the client's realisation
of his rights and satisfaction of his needs, there is a real tension
between employee status and professional obligation.

That tension is specifically addressed in the BASW Code. It
accepts that social workers should not impose on themselves
obligations which they are unable to fulfil, but refers to the 'right
and duty to bring to the attention of those in power and of the
general public, ways in which the activities of government, society
or agencies, create or contribute to hardship or suffering or
militate against their relief' (BASW 1975). Silence in the face of
injustice, or passive acquiescence in harmful policies are the

ethical offences in these terms. The political realities of employee status are therefore recognised while a professional responsibility is retained.

Practice within a bureaucratic structure presents difficulties as identified by Rhodes. It may be helpful to take a specific example – child sexual abuse – and examine the latent conflicts between organisational responses and a professional response. The high profile given to child sexual abuse following the development of Childline and the Cleveland inquiry places pressures on management from the DHSS to devise appropriate organisational models, from elected members to safeguard the authority from adverse publicity, from the media to act decisively to protect children at risk, and from staff to offer relevant training, consultation and support in this highly charged area of practice. The nature of response to these pressures will vary from authority to authority, but each source of pressure can be seen as potentially destructive of social work values.

Departmental concern for organisational solutions can cause confusion about the location of responsibility. The police, the paediatrician, the GP, the health visitor and the social worker all have separate roles. But consensus offers protection. In an area where all professionals feel acutely aware of their vulnerability to external criticism and scrutiny, there may be a tendency to fudge decision-making in the interests of achieving agreement. The exclusion of those directly concerned from that decision-making, for parental attendance at case conferences is still the exception, calls into question 'respect for clients as individuals' and the social worker's responsibility 'to ensure that their dignity, individuality, rights and responsibility shall be safeguarded' (BASW 1975).

The understandable pressure from elected members to protect the interests of the local authority can lead to an upward pull of decision-making responsibility with some decisions being taken only at Area Officer level. And there is a danger that imposed requirements dictating frequency of visiting, regularity of physical checks, and so on, may impair the worker's ability to respond to the client as an individual. This is not to deny the appropriateness of departmental prescriptions on occasion, but safeguards have a price in terms of personal professional responsibility.

The media pressure is an increasingly significant factor in some agencies. Where a person has a previous history of offences against children, has served a period of imprisonment and seeks to return home to a family with children, difficult decisions have to be taken. They go to the heart of social workers' views about the capacity for improvement and change of every individual, and also to the balancing act between the rights of children to protection from abuse and exploitation and the rights of the adult individual. The impact of media pressure has led to some departments taking up rigid stances, formulating guidelines using words like 'never' and 'in no circumstances' which actually vitiate the power of social workers to make an independent and objective judgement. Again it would be wrong to exaggerate the extent of these guidelines, but defensive social work practice may not be practice in tune with the values of social work.

The anxiety which staff experience in such situations should not be underestimated. One reaction is to seek shared decision-making. Primary care teams, senior social workers consultation, case conferences and reviews are all devices for spreading infor-mation and also, by implication, responsibility. The devices are legitimate but their impact on practice is again to blur a personal sense of obligation.

Horne (1987), in a clear analysis of the relationship between local authority social work and the values held by the profession, points out that the degree to which any worker can follow the prescriptions of the Code of Ethics is itself determined by the function of the employing agency. 'It exists under social auspices and as such its clients and its role with them is sanctioned and determined by society through agency function.' (Horne 1987, p. 93)

In summary therefore, the effect of these various organisational pressures is to reduce the sharpness and clarity of the personal Code of Ethics supported by professional associations, by diffusing the sense of personal obligation and responsibility. That diffusion is designed to help practitioners to comply with agency guidelines and policy, and to cope with the external pressures upon them. It leads, however, to a world far removed from the model of the self-regulating professional which underlies the Code.

Race and Gender

The last decade has seen an increasing emphasis in the public sector on race and gender issues. Official Government policy has supported concepts of racial and sexual equality and backed them by bodies like the Commission for Racial Equality and the Equal Opportunities Commission. Translating those concepts into reality has not been achieved by legislative prescription or liberal rhetoric. Some local authorities, initially those on the Left but increasingly spanning the political spectrum, have established separate Committee or Working Party structures to address the implications for the organisation and delivery of services of race and gender, and social work practice is slowly coming to address these issues. The importance now attached to these issues challenges the individualistic perspective of the Codes of Ethics.

The failure of traditional liberal perspectives adequately to deal with race issues is well described by Cheetham (1982). Treating every vulnerable individual in need in exactly the same way sounds an impossible response. Social workers frequently assert that they take no account of sex or colour in reaching decisions about services. Yet this colour-blind approach ignores totally the different cultural patterns in minority communities on matters like child-rearing patterns and the role of women in family life. It ignores totally the impact of racism on the attitudes and expectations of those from minority communities. This was expressly recognised in race relations legislation in the concept of indirect discrimination whereby a condition or requirement applied equally to different racial groups can be discriminatory in its effects on minority groups when the proportion of people in that group able to comply with the condition is considerably smaller than the proportion of persons in the population as a whole. Thus allocation of nursery places giving priority to single parents will effectively exclude Asian families, as will allocation policies giving a major weighting to length of residence in the local authority area.

The area of practice in which liberal attitudes have been challenged most vigorously is that of transracial fostering and adoption. The colour-blind approach is most clearly defective here for while black and mixed race children are frequently placed with white substitute parents, there are few if any instances of white children placed with black fosterparents. Black foster-parents are a scarce resource, but the reasons for the lack of such placements are not related only to scarcity. Racial matching is now widely accepted as desirable in preserving a child's ethnic heritage, in assisting in the development of a proper sense of identity, and in better equipping children to cope with discrimination.

Special needs require a special response, but tailoring services to reflect the multicultural nature of society still touches a raw nerve in many social workers, who react in a hostile way to what they regard as positive discrimination and thus subversive of considerations of equity. Similarly the ideological overtones which have surrounded the debate on transcultural placements have challenged the basis of usual judgements. Is it better to place a black child with a white substitute family rather than allow the child to languish in residential care? Is an indifferent black substitute family placement better for a black child than a good white family placement? Social policy considerations might come into conflict with the interests of the child, and social workers are forced into difficult ethical dilemmas by rigid local authority stances opposed to transracial placements when the evidence of the outcomes of such placements is surprisingly positive (Gill and Jackson 1982).

This issue facing workers is whether considerations of ethnicity should be paramount in such placements. Without taking an absolutist stance prohibiting transracial placements, workers need to be aware of the significance of institutional racism and to be aware of their own prejudices before reaching a view.

Just as race issues can pose a challenge to the liberal individualism characteristic of most social work value positions so too can gender issues. 'Social work concepts and practice are so loosely linked to concepts of family roles and responsibilities that the challenge to social work is more fundamental than to any other social service' (Moore 1986, p. 66).

The structure of social institutions reflects the patriarchal nature of society. Day-care provision reflects societal value judgements about a woman's place, and the structure of support systems available for carers also reflect assumptions about the caring role being taken by females. The move to community care has been criticised (Finch and Groves 1983) because of the implicit assumption that families – meaning women – should take greater responsibility for their vulnerable members.

The implication of eliminating gender discrimination in society is a radical recasting of those social roles with caring ceasing to be a predominantly female role, and with men and women taking up roles by choice and aptitude rather than as a result of social expectations and pressures. As with racism, one can see that a sensitivity to gender issues may cause the social worker to challenge the established order in a way which will cause discomfort to the employing agency, and possibly to the family where traditional roles have operated in a way to exploit the female members. Awareness of the social issues involved has forced some social workers to look to a Marxist analysis rather than seek a reconciliation with the mainstream values of social work.

The Radical Critique

In a forceful assault on social work values, Simpkin noted 'a positive affirmation of the united nuclear family as the deepest source of human emotional satisfaction, and a tendency to judge people's emotional capacity by their ability to adapt to family life' (Simpkin 1979, p. 28) and described the social worker's world as a 'soggy web of reciprocal obligations and damp responses which is founded more on respect for institutions than a realistic appraisal of personal need' (p. 29).

As mediators between State and the public, social workers have licensed freedom providing they operate within the value system of the State. This view of the State, Simpkin recognises, depends on an analysis of society derived from Marx in contrast to the pluralist view of the State as the guardian of the public interest and individual views in a society composed of competing interest groups.

A Marxist perspective would therefore reject the individualist emphasis of the value systems used in social work practice, and would also reject the role accorded to work by social work viewing that as an illustration of the central role accorded to production within capitalism. The trends within social security legislation which seek to stigmatise claimants, and to link the receipt of benefits to 'training' programmes or 'community work', can be seen as mechanisms to reinforce the mode of production.

A key concept would be the recognition of the working-class experience of struggle and subordination, and thus the necessity of building on collective links between organisations. As State employees, 'social workers can both enhance and negate human welfare within the same processes of their work' (Corrigan and Leonard 1978, p. 106) by securing short-term improvements in individual well-being while providing a soothing lotion to the problems created by capitalism. An analysis of the triangular relationship between the state, social work and the working class has to recognise the view of 'working class communities who experience their relationship with social workers and the local welfare apparatus predominantly as control, subordination and incorporation − a relationship more likely to be characterised by antagonism than partnership' (Leonard 1983).

This picture of social work is fundamentally different from the liberal democratic consensus view of the welfare state. It emphasises the social system rather than individual pathology as the root cause of social problems. It is suspicious of both managerial authority and of professionalism, regarding both as taking away the power of the client. It rejects social work involvement in social control functions and it is sceptical of the emphasis placed on the nuclear family as the basis for intervention.

Yet there is no consensus within the radical critique about the way to reconcile the role of the welfare worker in the public sector. Simpkin (1983), Jones (1983) and Corrigan and Leonard (1978) offer differing prescriptions of the strategy to be followed. Like much social work practice, their analysis of the problems is far more persuasive than the treatment strategy set out.

The dilemma of how to work within a system which one is seeking to change is, however, not confined to those who follow a Marxist analysis. Many subscribers to the liberal democratic model would also assert a commitment to social change, and to redressing the inequalities now prevailing in society. As has been seen, the Codes of Ethics do not offer any answers about respective responsibilities to promote social change and to operate as an employee. The radical analysis is helpful in highlighting social work's socially legitimated role as mediating established values and working to promote and preserve the family, the work ethic and individual solutions to problems. But it is too dismissive in its treatment of professionalism, for the Codes of Ethics could be developed and adapted as instruments challenging both managerialism and bureaucracy.

The New Professionalism

The most coherent exposition of the new professionalism has come from Cypher (1986). The inspiration for a new approach came from an address by Bill Jordan to BASW's Anual Conference in Edinburgh in 1975. The title he adopted, 'Clients are fellow citizens', was used as the title of a BASW working party report (1980), which explored how clients rights could assume a central place in social work practice, how participation in case conferences and reviews could be developed and how empowerment of clients could be made a reality.

Central to this evolution of policy was the concept of citizenship and the entitlement of clients to the rights of citizens. Borrowing language from the consumer movement, the concept of citizenship in social work entails questions of access, of information, of complaints and redress and of participation. It is built on the foundation that every citizen is entitled to be involved in the decision-making processes of social work, to have the opportunity to be heard and to appeal against decisions taken. The professional, fortified by possession of an exclusive knowledge and skill, taking decisions in the best interests of the client is wholly alien to this approach. The new professionalism does not deny the existence of that knowledge and skill but seek to bridge the gap between worker and client, and to widen the range of choices open to the client.

There is nothing in this approach which is at variance with the practice guidelines implicit in the Code of Ethics, but there is a reinterpretation which addresses some criticisms. First, while there is still the inbuilt construction of problem situations in terms of individual pathology, there is a determined effort to locate the client in a collective context by extending to the client rights shared by all. Second, there is a conscious attempt to address the imbalance of power between worker and client by the provision of information, and by establishing processes whereby clients' views can be heard.

Three examples of the process can illustrate the benefits, but also the limitations, inherent in the sharing of power. They are record-keeping, complaints procedures, and participation in case conferences.

Record-keeping

In 1983 the British Association of Social Workers published *Effective and Ethical Recording* (BASW 1983). This addressed the ethical issues in record-keeping practice, and highlighted the way in which the client was deprived of the opportunity even to know what was being written within the agency, and certainly to see and challenge the record. Having identified widespread recognition of the labelling and stereotyping contained within social services files, and the verbosity of some file entries wholly concealing the existence of any plan for work with the client, the paper called for the establishment of a new system of recording practice. The records would be shared with the client at the time of the interview, the client's comments would be recorded, and the content of the record should be limited to factual, verifiable material with opinion clearly separated and described as such.

At the same time as the BASW Working Party, a young Liverpool man, Gordon Gaskin, was seeking access to the file held by the local authority on his life in care. The DHSS issued a circular (DHSS 1984) giving guidance to local authorities on access, and urging them to adopt procedures which would provide access to clients with a right of appeal in the event of their request for access being denied. The circular provided for exceptions to access where it would be detrimental to the client, or prejudice the interests of third parties.

Local authorities with varying degrees of enthusiasm have adopted procedures. With all the limitations and exemptions, the procedures do represent a major advance for clients – an advance which owes much to the influence and advocacy of the new professionalism without which it is unlikely that either the DHSS or local authorities would have been willing to cede as much influence to client interests.

Complaints procedures

The assumption that professional power would be exercised in the best interests of clients has meant that social services authorities have been slow to establish formal procedures whereby complaints could be processed. The need for complaints procedures challenges not only that assumption, but also the adequacy of representative democracy as a safeguard of consumer interests. In theory, dissatisfied users of personal social services have the same rights as those aggrieved with the conduct of other local authority services. They can seek the assistance of the local councillor to channel their complaint. In practice, the majority of users of personal social services lack the confidence to approach local councillors, who are sometimes themselves seen as figures of authority within the community. When they do approach councillors, they may not always be able to frame their grievances in ways which readily lend themselves to councillor investigation.

Notwithstanding the lack of initial enthusiasm from professionals and politicians, there have been some moves to formalise complaints procedures with child-care services producing much of the impetus for change. The National Consumer Council (NCC 1988) and BASW (1988) have both produced carefully argued cases recommending procedures which provide an independent element in the investigation of complaints, which seek to create a climate in which agencies do not regard complaints as a threat, and which offer support to potential complainants in articulating and preparing their grounds of complaint. While this may seem paternalistic, the offer of assistance is necessary if clients are not to be deterred by the inevitable formality of agency procedures.

Professionalism is an important factor here in promoting client interests, for trade unions are often unhappy at the establishment of procedures which leave staff vulnerable to unfounded or malicious complaints. Striking the balance is difficult but the right to be heard is a fundamental element of citizenship. Supporters of the new professionalism who identify with the client as consumer need to continue to assert that right and to ensure that accessible complaints procedures are available for all client groups.

Case conference and reviews

The call from *Clients are Fellow Citizens* for consumers of social services to participate in decisions about their future evoked a ready response from practitioners. It is now commonplace to find young people in care contributing to their reviews, to see day-

centre attenders involved in planning and evaluating their own
programmes, and to find in homes for the elderly a range of
devices from residents' committees to advocacy schemes designed
to strengthen participation and involvement. Working with clients
rather than for them involves learning new skills, but more and
more workers are demonstrating their readiness to work openly
with clients.

While most social workers unequivocally accept and welcome
client involvement there are much greater divergences of view
about the best way to structure this without creating false expectations. Decision-making power tends to remain firmly with the professionals with the client's views being heard, but not necessarily in
the decision-making phase of reviews and conferences. The attitudes
of other professionals can also serve as a constraint especially in
child abuse case conferences where much information is ex-
changed under a cloak of confidentiality, and both police and
medical personnel argue that the presence of parents would inhibit
free discussion and prejudice the exchange of information. Yet
parents have a right both to express their views to the case
conference, a right stressed in the recommendations in the Cleveland enquiry, and to know the decisions taken and the reasons for
them. Various models are being developed to give parents the
chance to join at least part of the case conference. And the
participative orientation of the new professionalism with its emphasis on the rights of clients has played a crucial role in that
process.

The way ahead

It will be clear that the new professionalism has been much
influenced in its turn by the more committed social action stance of
radical social workers. The legitimacy of social change as a
preoccupation of social workers to stand alongside individual work
has been codified in the ethical prescriptions of professional
associations. Race and gender issues are being incorporated into
discussions about ethics as the profession takes a wider view of its
social values. Yet the very concept of professionalism is still alien
to many social workers, as has been discussed above.

What appears to be emerging twenty years after the publication
of the Seebohm Report is an occupational group, larger in size and

power than ever before in social work, but whose values and ideals are under attack from two sides. First, the Victorian values espoused by the Thatcher Government and reflected in social policy changes are not those with which social workers readily identify – work is often an aspiration incapable of attainment, thrift is impossible on social security benefit levels, and self-help is a difficult plant to cultivate in environments characterised by hopelessness and powerlessness. Second the monopolistic position enjoyed by local authorities as employers of social workers has led them into a stance of opposition to social work's professional aspirations, which could threaten the dominant role employers occupy in relation to entry to social work and conditions of employment.

Despite these pressures, there has been a consistent strand of debate about the desirability of a register of social workers with professional qualifications. The Joint Steering Group on Accreditation produced in 1977 a paper entitled *The Future of Social Work* which proposed the establishment of a General Social Work Council to accredit courses of training in social work, of individual social work practitioners, and to regulate practice through disciplinary procedures. The Steering Group report, backed by all the professional associations except the National Association of Probation Officers, represented something of a highwater mark for proponents of a traditional professionalism. A combintion of BASW's internal financial difficulties, the advent of the Thatcher Government with a radical social policy agenda, and the failure to persuade the Barclay Committee of the practicability of the Council, meant that the next five years saw little concerted pressure exercised in favour of the Council.

The issue of registration has again assumed a higher profile. There are three reasons for this. First, the monopoly position of local authority employers is being eroded. Second, there is growing concern about the competence of social workers and how best to ensure minimum standards. Third, there is a recognition within social work that local authority employers cannot always be trusted to uphold professional standards.

The erosion of monopoly power is not a development widely welcomed within social work, for it reflects the determined thrust of Government policy towards a plural system of welfare with an enhanced role for the private and voluntary sectors in the spectrum of provision. While it would remain true that the great majority of social worker posts are still in the public sector, the voluntary sector is increasingly moving into direct service provision. Through housing associations, local support groups for mentally handicapped people and those with mental health problems are providing accommodation and day-care support. Specialist national bodies concerned with particular types of disability – the Spastics Society, the Royal National Institute for the Blind, and the Royal National Institute for the Deaf – are moving from a lobbying role to one which includes an element of direct service. The private sector, fuelled by the social security funding available, has moved to dominate the provision of residential care of the elderly and is looking for new areas of expansion. As social workers move into these settings, a vigorous professionalism is an attractive protection for staff in offering an external basis for setting standards.

The spate of inquiries into child care issues shows little sign of abating, and raises issues of professional competence. Training, supervision, recordkeeping have all been subject to critical scrutiny. The need for a longer period of training is well recognised but the key issue is the nature and availability of support available to staff after they have been qualified and appointed. Here the concept of an independent assessment of competence in practice through a scheme of accreditation can be viewed as an attractive additional safeguard. It is intriguing to note that social work stands alone among the health and welfare professions in having no system of statutory regulation of practice.

This decade has seen a marked shift in long-held attitudes in some local authorities. The mutual respect, and recognised demarcation of roles between members and officers, have come under challenge, with members asserting their right to intervene in professional decision-making. It has often been sensitive issues of race and sexual orientation on which professionals have had their judgement challenged. The vivid description in the Tyra Henry report (Lambeth 1987) of 'poisonous' relationships between social services committee members and officers indicates the depths of mistrust which can be generated. When this does happen, an external guarantor of standards like the General Social Work Council can be a valuable protector of public interests.

The concept of self-regulation does, however, have its critics, and not just among those who deny the existence of a recognisable and distinctive corpus of social work knowledge. It is challenged as applying a nineteenth-century model of professional self-regulation without regard to the public interest to what is quintessentially a late twentieth-century profession. The Association of Directors of Social Services in their document specifically addressed this point: 'there is great concern that any Council should not be viewed as a self-serving professional oligarchy. The importance of strong, independent consumer and public representatives is therefore recognised' (ADSS, 1986). The preferred model espoused by the ADSS borrowed heavily from the nursing profession, which has developed a model of regulation by the United Kingdom Central Council and the National Boards, by proposing a Council with one-third of its members to be appointed by the Secretary of State to represent employer and consumer interests.

One concern is that a Council would focus on social work to the exclusion of other occupational groups within social services. Once again the tension between local authority employment and professional status is evident with a resistance to linking registration to qualifications rather than to employment status. Given the continuing divisions within social work's own representative bodies, is the notion of the Council one of those ideas destined never to proceed beyong the discussion stage? There are some grounds for thinking that, while the Council will not be achieved easily, there is a real prospect of progress. Breaking the monopoly position of local authority employment is unequivocally recommended in the Griffiths Report, and setting up professional power as a countervailing influence to local authorities' current dominance could be attractive options in the political context of a Conservative administration.

The most likely scenario for achieving a Council is paradoxically a negative one. Blom-Cooper's report into the Kimberly Carlisle case (1987) indicated support for the notion of greater professional self-regulation. Social work's professionalism has been subject to more intense scrutiny than that of any other occupational group, and the scrutiny has found social work too often wanting in terms of its clarity about professional standards. Sadly, a scandal in a politically motivated authority is more likely to bring about leverage in social policy than is professional lobbying and

influence. But without external regulation and clearly defined standards of professional conduct, the sensitive balance of competing
rights is likely to be viewed by members as part of their legitimate
sphere of influence.

4

Education and Training

The debate within social work education about the DSW (Diploma in Social Work) and the Certificate in Social Care has a ring of familiarity to those who have followed the arguments in social work stretching over the last four decades. History may have its lessons for future generations, but this presupposes an ability and readiness to learn from past mistakes – and that is not always evident from the tenor and content of some of the arguments surrounding the future direction of education and training for social work. The use of education and training as related but separate concepts is deliberate, for that has been and remains the battleground for conflicting views about course content, values and course organisation.

The Seebohm Report was unequivocal in its call for 'staff trained in the principles and skills that are common to all forms of social work with individuals and families' (Seebohm, para. 531, 1968) and described the separate system of specialist trainings which existed at the time as 'educationally and professionally unsound' and 'an indefensible waste of scarce resources which should not continue' (para. 533). The conclusion drawn was that there should be one central body responsible for promoting the training of staff in personal social services. The Government accepted this recommendation, and drew together the responsibilities of the three existing councils in the Central Council for Education and Training in Social Work in 1971. With its advent the specialist courses came to an end and 'were reconstructed to provide a basic qualification for professional social work with less emphasis on a particular setting' (CCETSW 1973).

The Certificate of Qualification in Social Work became the recognised qualification for social work. Two pressures characterised the early years of the new Council. First, there was a period of unprecedented change and growth in personal social services. Expansion – and rapid expansion – of training places was required to meet the apparently insatiable demand of local authority social services for trained manpower. Maintaining quality is a major problem when volume is the yardstick by which success is measured. Some of the courses approved were indifferent with inexperienced teaching staff. The second pressure was to address the even more acute deficits in training for residential and day care staffing. It is important to trace the nature of the response to that pressure which remains unmet fifteen years on, for it contains the seeds of later dissension.

A CCETSW Working Party on Education for Residential Social Work (CCETSW 1973) distinguished between social work and welfare work, and argued that this should be reflected in a two-tier pattern of training, with social workers obtaining the CQSW and welfare workers the Certificate of Qualification in Welfare Work with the former qualification being superior in status and a necessary precondition for appointment to senior posts. The aversion of social work to elitism has been noted previously, and the proposals produced considerable criticism. A second version of the report produced in the light of consultation (CCETSW 1974) boldly asserted, *Residential Work is Part of Social Work*. Most work in residential settings was social work, and what could be differentiated was the level of skill required for competence in particular roles rather than different types of work. A Certificate of Proficiency in Social Work was proposed to replace the Welfare Work qualification.

The need for a different form of training, less academic in its orientation and more closely geared to the performance of tasks in the employment setting, was widely recognised in view of the manpower pressures being experienced. But whether that training was for different types of work, or different levels of work, remained a fatal ambiguity. By September 1974, the CCETSW announced its intention to introduce a new type of training in social service leading to the Certificate in Social Service. The nomenclature suggests that work of a different character from that of social work was envisaged, and social work was specifically excluded from CSS curricula. But CSS was not envisaged as a different level of qualification. Borrowing from the 1944 Education Act, 'equal but different' was the phrase in vogue.

Three months after CCETSW's decision, a DHSS Working Party met for the first time to consider the need for trained manpower in the personal social services. By the time it reported in 1976, its expansionist recommendations were notably out of tune with the temper of the times as the Labour Government engaged on a drastic retrenchment of public spending. The Birch Report (DHSS 1976) sought a position by the mid-eighties in which roughly half the staff employed would hold either CSS or CQSW qualifications.

Despite the expansionist tenor of the report, it was explicit on the debate between quality and quantity. 'If quality is to improve, quantity will have to hold back at least for a few years while investment in training is increased' (DHSS 1976, p. 11). Holding back was hardly what happened. CSS schemes never reached the assumed intake of 9000 students per annum, nor did CQSW ever expand to the annual intake of 6000 students assumed. The do-nothing scenario in the Birch Report included for comparative purposes only has come closest to reality.

The Report did make a bold stab at the desirable ratio between CQSW and CSS, did clearly identify social work tasks in residential and day care settings, and did attempt to differentiate roles which should be performed by a CQSW holder. These were circumstances involving loss of liberty or a change of home for the client, compulsorily or voluntarily, and situations demanding complex assessment or treatment/planning.

A vigorous debate followed the publication of the Birch Report, less on the training aspirations, which it was swiftly evident would remain just that, than on the differentiation of roles proposed in the report. Once again the word elitism was used as a boo-word to decry the legitimacy of any such attempt to distinguish staff roles by qualification. BASW's paper *The Social Work Task* (BASW 1977) fuelled the flames by developing further the categorisation suggested by the Birch Report, and proposing the following criteria for deciding whether the skills of a qualified social worker were required:

(a) level of client vulnerability – physical, psychological and social;
(b) degree of case complexity;
(c) significance of decision-making.

Three strands need to be distinguished in the opposition voiced to the approach favoured in the two reports. First, there was a resistance to drawing artificial dividing lines between clients on the basis of their needs in terms of allocating work. The tyranny of the case meant that workers, having initiated contact, were very reluctant to pass the case on to another worker if the issues became more complex or significant. Secondly, social workers in both residential and fieldwork settings found themselves performing exactly the same tasks as their unqualified colleagues and experiencing the same difficulties. They were unable or unwilling to claim superior competence in their performance of their work. Thirdly, the steadily increasing number of CSS holders brought a different, more practical orientation to their work which was immediately attractive to management. It also created a lobby group within social services resistant to any concept of an elite group of social workers occupying senior positions.

The Barclay Committee also had to look at the issue of task differentiation, given its terms of reference – which were 'to review the role and tasks of social workers in local authority social services departments and related voluntary agencies'. Predictably the Committee noted the disproportionate allocation of qualified staff to child-care cases, work with families with multiple problems or people with a mental handicap or mental illness while unqualified staff carried more cases of physically handicapped and elderly people. In setting out a potential list of situations where social work help was indicated, the Committee borrowed from both Birch and BASW in identifying:

* life and liberty are at risk
* a major change of living situation may be involved
* counselling may be needed when private sorrows or relationship problems are escalating into life crisis proportions
* the client, family or group seems unable to make use of available resources
* a network of resources needs to be established and monitored.

If an elderly person has problems of these kinds, we consider they are as much in need of social work help as a child might be.

We cannot accept what is in effect rationing by age (Barclay 1982, p. 47).

However, Barclay went on to identify tasks which social workers should not be doing, and which could be performed by other staff, other agencies or by volunteers. The examples cited were:

* routine clerical work
* arranging transport or payment for transport for clients
* assessing routine requests for assistance
* assessing the need for and issuing aids for the disabled
* much routine provision of practical aid and advice, surveillance and monitoring
* systematic provision of information and advice
* routine assessment of housing need
* rent collection
* debt collecting for fuel/water boards.

(Barclay 1982, p. 51)

Had the Report ended at that point, it would have performed a helpful public service by providing a basis for restructuring the delivery of local authority social services in a way which established a clear division between tasks for qualified staff and tasks for unqualified staff. But the central recommendation of the Report for community social work, and the emotional and personalised debate which ensued, following the two notes of dissent and reservation by Professors Hadley and Pinker, served to cloak the significance of the Committee's earlier work in clarifying social work tasks.

The argument developed in the two notes was far more fundamental, for it went to the core of the value systems to be deployed in looking at social work. In this section, the difference of emphasis on training is of critical significance. Professor Hadley and his colleagues challenged the 'professional' orientation of the main body of the report. While stopping short of rejecting the need for trained staff, their note comments that 'social services departments and social workers rate knowledge, training, qualifications and skill highly while clients, not underrating these, put personal qualities much higher. . . . Experience, sensitivity, integrity, commitment are among the most highly-rated qualities clients look for in social workers' (Barclay 1982, p. 226). From this, the argument was developed for a blurring of roles between social workers, social work assistants and neighbourhood workers.

Pinker takes a diametrically opposed view, vigorously challenging the idea of applying egalitarian principles to standards of knowledge and skill; that, he thinks, is an intellectual exercise which goes unchallenged because the majority of social work clients are poor and powerless. 'If the characteristic patterns of risk and dependency confronting social workers were to spread to the majority of the population, the general public would very soon demand services of the highest quality from professional social workers of the highest calibre' (Barclay 1982, p. 258). The possibility of opportunities for CSS holders to convert their qualification into a CQSW was welcomed as sensible, but in a prescient note Pinker asserted that it would be 'pointless if, in deference to egalitarianism, the roles, tasks and status of the two qualifications were to be made virtually identical' (Barclay 1982, p. 261).

Yet such moves were underway, although not fully articulated as such. CCETSW initiated a review of qualifying training policies which, when published (CCETSW 1983), indicated widespread support for discontinuing the separation of the two types of training although there was little agreement about the best way forward. Discussion about the way in which progress could be made occupied the next three years, being caught up in a wider debate about the future of social work training at university level as the financial stringencies forced on the University Grants Committee necessitated some CQSW course closures. The continued practicability of two-year training was also questioned in view of the increasing demands on social workers.

As an illustration of the Murphy's Law theory it could scarcely be bettered. The combination of a desire to move to three-year training with a single qualifying award (decisions taken in September 1985) meant that decisions about the CQSW/CSS issue were taken almost as a sub-issue to the major debate about the shape and location of the proposed new Qualifying Diploma in Social Work. A further decision to regard the two qualifications as equivalent after the advent of QDSW meant that for all practical purposes, CSS had become a social work qualification almost by inadvertence. A programme set up for different staff groups doing different types of work, specifically excluded from teaching social work, had achieved full professional recognition. The end result is an undoubted tribute to the quality of CSS schemes. It was also influenced by the strong management lobby welcoming the opportunity to be directly involved in controlling course content. But it is an even more eloquent testimony of the continuing failure of social work, its professional bodies, and its practitioners to define what differentiated social work from other forms of intervention.

Just as, twenty years earlier, the architects of the Younghusband courses had not anticipated that their course would have the same qualification status as the university-based courses in applied social studies, so too the initiators of CSS schemes had failed to anticipate the strength of the egalitarian instincts within social work.

The QDSW

The problems of cramming a quart into the pint pot of social work training in two years had long been recognised. They received authoritative backing from the House of Commons Select Committee in 1983/1984, and the Jasmine Beckford inquiry report (Beckford 1985), both of which had called for an extension of social work training to three years. CCETSWW determined to move forward on the basis of a variety of different routes to the qualification from two-year programmes for a minority of graduate entrants whose previous course of study was directly relevant to social work, four-year degree courses and three-year programmes for the great majority of students, some of which would be employment-based and some of which would be linked to an educational qualification (CCETSW 1987a).

The mode of developing programmes borrowed heavily from CSS schemes, with a collaborative relationship envisaged between educational institutions and employing agencies. A delicate balance between the generic approach and the development of specialist skills was struck with the requirement that every student would be expected to develop an area of special emphasis related to client groups, settings or social work methods.

In its case to the Government for funding, CCETSW said bluntly that the existing qualifications had failed

> to keep pace with demands created by the massive changes which have occurred
> * in legislation (62 Acts of Parliament since 1972 have particular significance for social work practice)
> * in national and agency policies
> * in patterns of service delivery, in particular the move to care in the community, and
> * in society itself, and in the nature and context of social needs contained within it (CCETSW 1987).

Had CCETSW stopped there one might have wished it well in its bid to the Government for financial assistance, but it went on to outline proposals for a Certificate in Social Care. It is difficult to resist the temptation to say that it already existed as the Certificate in Social Service. It is important to look critically at what was proposed, since it became the focus of controversy. It was greeted sceptically by those in social care who feared second-class status, by other groups resisting CCETSW's attempt to take a leadership role and by those who questioned the analysis leading to the recommendation.

The National Council for Vocational Qualifications works in conjunction with Industry Lead Bodies to define the skills and competencies required at various levels. It has a system of skill levels, which were tested by a Working Group on Manpower Planning against the needs of social work and social care employment. This produced an estimate of 425 000 posts in total in Britain of which 280 000 were thought to require level 2 skills, 59 000 level 3 and 24 000 level 4. To address this need, CCETSW decided to institute a new qualification – the Certificate in Social Care – while leaving open whether this should be a single award or modular in form building up from one level to another. The target group designated was described as 'the growing group of ancillary staff in the probation service supervising community service orders, social work assistants providing practical support to elderly clients, home helps, care assistants in residential and day care settings, and many more' (CCETSW 1987b).

QDSW is regarded as a level 5 qualification so a CSC at level 3 could be regarded also as the entry requirement for a three-year QDSW programme, while a level 4 award could provide exemption from all or part of the first year of such a course, or provide access to a two-year programme. The proposed start date for these proposals was 1991.

It is churlish to criticise proposals directed at addressing a longstanding deficit in the provision of training for social care. The scale of the need is such that bold proposals are required, and the collaboration involved in the Lead Industry Body mechanism should ensure a concerted attack on the backlog. But looking at the past twenty years' piecemeal development of training, there are grounds for concern that insufficient analysis has been undertaken of the needs of the staff groups involved and that issues of status are again being left unresolved.

From the above discussion in relation to CSS and its eventual acceptance as 'equivalent' to CQSW, one can identify three warning signals. First, there is still no clear and agreed differentiation between the social work task and that of social work assistants. Those social work assistants who have obtained a CSS qualification will seek full professional and financial recognition as social workers, yet their tasks will remain indistinguishable from those of staff without a qualification. When social work assistants acquire a level 3 or level 4 CSC, the pressure for equal treatment with CSS holders will be hard to resist. Employers will not adopt a consistent approach to task differentiation according to qualification. Despite Birch, BASW, and Barclay, CCETSW's proposals continue to ignore this issue and are likely in 10 years time to produce a repeat of this decade's discussions about CSS and CQSW, and the discussions two decades earlier about the Certificate in Social Work courses.

Secondly, care assistants in residential and day care settings are suggested as suitable candidates for CSC courses. The sheer size of the training deficit in residential and day care work will make CSC an attractive option to employers, but again the proposed system ignores the years of discussion about caring roles in residential settings. There is considerable difficulty in separating out the skills of staff in a home, all of whom will at different times be involved in the direct provision of care for residents including counselling. While there are legitimate managerial skills, they will not be taught on QDSW courses. Strip away those management roles and it is difficult to distinguish conceptually between the work of the Officer in Charge and other members of the care staff as residential facilities are currently organised. Unless there are moves to extend the responsibility of social work staff to cover roles traditionally associated with fieldwork, one can foresee a repetition of the CSS/CQSW debate. The Wagner Report (1988, p. 87) accepted that at all levels in residential work there are elements of social work and accordingly recommended that there should be no rigid distinction between the content of QDSW and CSC. Yet if no such distinction is drawn, the seeds of future problems will be sown even before the courses come into being. There is a world of difference between encouraging and facilitating transfer and progression from one course to the other, and denying the existence of any major distinction between the two.

Thirdly, there is, as has been noted previously, a continuing strand of egalitarianism in social work which rejects the assumed linkage of qualifications and higher levels of skill and knowledge. This is backed by traditional trade union attitudes which believe in the rate for the job regardless of qualifications held, and which have been influential in resisting moves to professionalise caring. The stratified concept of the NCVQ with QDSW at the top of the qualifications hierarchy is undoubtedly going to be challenged by proponents of the patch concept who favour the blurring of fieldwork roles.

There exists therefore a number of anxieties about possible scenario which could develop. These can be considered under the headings of resources, realism and reluctance.

Resources

The original CCETSW proposals envisaged an additional expenditure on QDSW in the region of 40 million pounds. This has to be seen in the context of current expenditure of £73 million on CSS and CQSW. The scale of the increase at a time of continuing pressure on public expenditure was undeniably ambitious. Despite a high profile and a well-orchestrated campaign to secure Government support, backed with unusual unanimity by all branches of the social welfare occupational spectrum, the eventual response of Government was not so much disappointing as derisory. Set against a bid for £40 million, the offer of one million pounds to undertake further work was a striking contrast to the positive response which had been given to the parallel moves to improve and extend qualifying training for nursing in the Project 2000 proposals. CCETSW has decided to go ahead with a two-year Diploma in Social Work plotted jointly with employment interests.

Realism

The costings for the Certificate in Social Care assumed a net additional cost of only 9 million pounds to achieve two-thirds of the staff trained at all levels within five years. Even more implausibly, it was assumed that with no increase in spending that target could be reached within a ten-year period. While CCETSW described their estimates as 'complex and necessarily tentative' (CCETSW 1987a), every favourable assumption seemed to be included in the costings. They assumed, for instance, that all existing in-service training would cease for these staff and that the resources would be transferred to CSC. They assumed that the existing Manpower Services Commission programmes constituted an adequate training for level 2, and that 25 per cent of the target numbers for this level will be trained in this way. Given the scale of training numbers, the costings were disproportionately low compared to the resources deployed on QDSW.

The lack of realism extends to the blinkered view of social work training in isolation from that of other related disciplines. The Audit Commission, in its discussion of training, noted with some justice that 'the problem is not knowing in general terms what needs to be done, but rather securing action at the national level' (Audit Commission 1986, p. 64). Its radical proposal, greeted with a deafening silence by all the professions, was:

> a basic training would lead initially to a basic grade 'community care worker' who could act as a generalist and main contact for people in the community. This basic training would need to be recognised by the various professional bodies, and to give advanced standing towards professional qualifications. Further specialist training (in occupational therapy, mental health, social work, etc.) could then be added, leading eventually to the various professional qualifications (Audit Commission, p. 76).

The Griffiths Report endorsed this concept seeing it as 'a development of the roles of some home helps/home care assistants, community nursing assistants and residential care staff' (Griffiths 1988, p. 25) and 'a multi-purpose auxiliary force to be given limited training and to give help of a practical nature in the field of community care' (p. ix). The ideas could be given reality through the NCVQ approach but all the professional bodies persist in developing their policies apparently in isolation from the other professions engaged in community care.

Reluctance

The reluctance is that of all the parties to the discussions on qualifying training – the Government, the training institutions, CCETSW, employing agencies, trade unions and professional associations – to grasp the nettle by making a series of clear, unambiguous statements about future training policy. Yet the very persistence of that reluctance, understandable as it is in terms of resources and the studied ambiguity required to secure agreement from a number of bodies with conflicting interests, threatens the success of the whole enterprise.

What statements then could resolve the ambiguity? They should reflect the lessons of the twenty years since Seebohm, and should set clear objectives for the remainder of the century. An alternative manifesto could be based on five clear statements:

1 Social work and group care are skilled activities which require appropriate training.
2 The continued use of unqualified staff in these roles is unacceptable, and will be ended by 2000 AD.
3 A hierarchy of training is both necessary and desirable, and certain posts should be reserved for those holding specified qualifications. (The Wagner Report argues that people filling managerial and senior positions in residential work require a full social work qualification.)
4 The designation 'social worker' should be restricted to those holding DSW or its equivalent.

5 A new Council combining education and training functions with those of professional regulation should be established to cover social workers.

The impact of such statements would be profound. The first might be thought to be unexceptionable, but it is in some ways the most radical. It requires first an acceptance that employing authorities have with the collusion of Government been employing staff in key caring roles for whom they have failed to provide adequate or appropriate training. But it also requires an acceptance that training does make a difference, and that a good heart and warm personality may be necessary conditions for the performance of caring roles but are not in themselves sufficient conditions. Many of the ideas set out by CCETSW in relation to CSC do provide for the development of a national framework. What is at issue is the commitment required to achieve it, which will necessitate a greater resource injection of time and funding than is currently recognised.

The corollary of that approach has to be an end to the recruitment and employment of unqualified staff. A target date is a useful discipline. It has worked successfully in education. It concentrates the mind. It shapes resource allocation, rather than resource allocation for ever pushing back the attainment of targets. The year 2000 – the beginning of a new millenium – has a stirring sense of promise. By its flabbiness about possible proportions of trained staff within five, ten or fifteen years, CCETSW has missed an opportunity to catch the imagination of those engaged in the enterprise of a massive upgrading of standards. Some of the training to be delivered will be in-service before full performance of caring roles, but – however generous the transitional protection for staff currently in post – the goal should be to include *all* staff within the framework. Fifteen years ago, a probation officer direct entrant was seconded on a two-year CQSW course at the age of 58. That sense of boldness, bravery and imagination will be required from employers to achieve the target.

The model developed by CCETSW (Figure 4.1) has considerable merits. Its main weaknesses are the uncertainties about the role of the Basic and Advanced Certificates in Social Care, and the failure to establish a prescribed level of qualification as a requirement for certain posts. This last is highly controversial. It is difficult

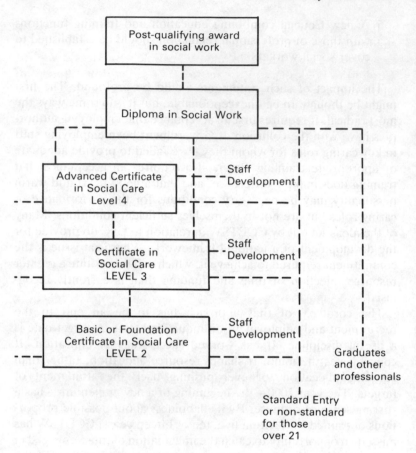

Figure 4.1 *Framework for the continuum of social care, social work and post-qualifying training*

to achieve because of the blurring of qualified and unqualified staff in virtually every occupational role in personal social services, and it will be resisted by trade unions. But until it is tackled, it is hard to see how many of the problems experienced in the past two decades will be resolved. What is needed is a definitive statement that all social workers will be required to hold a DSW or equivalent, that all holders of senior positions in residential settings should be required to have a DSW or equivalent, that all staff in caring roles which involve counselling (that is, all in children's homes, mental health settings, and most mental handicap settings, and many in elderly people's services), will be required to hold a Certificate in Social Care, and that those staff who work in group care settings but whose work consists of what Parker has termed 'tending' – the physical care of vulnerable individuals – should have in-service training to specified standards (broadly equivalent to level 2 of the NCVQ category).

The protection of title in restricting the designation 'social worker' to those with a qualification is an integral part of the package proposed. This would have two main benefits – one professional and the other political. Professionally, it would be an important statement about the precondition of qualifying training. But politically it would be even more important, in tackling one of the problems which beset social work, since the phrase is widely used to cover all aspects of helping work with vulnerable individuals.

To consolidate and reinforce the protection of title, a regulatory body is required. Some of the arguments for a Council of this kind were rehearsed in the previous chapter. In the context of education and training, however, it is important to note that the structure and strategy proposed here, and designed to enforce and strengthen the role of qualifications, have to be counterbalanced by a scheme of accreditation. Completion of a DSW will not in itself produce a fully competent worker, and needs to be buttressed by external assessment of practice standards leading to entry on a register of accredited workers.

This fivefold approach builds on the work already undertaken by CCETSW, but seeks to give it more of a cutting edge. It would reinforce the position of social work as the lead profession within the personal social services, but would do so in the context of the broader definition of social work implicit in the DSW structure. It would also provide impetus to the development of post qualification training.

Post-qualification training is one of the casualties of the general financial situation facing social services and educational establishments. The absence of any recognised advanced training was recognised in the sixties, but it took a further ten years before CCETSW in 1975 set out its proposals. The discussions were characterised by the 'familiar tensions between the demands of practice, research and the quality of social work teaching *vis-à-vis* academic disciplines' (Younghusband 1978, p. 59). The CCETSW proposals (CCETSW 1975 a,b) envisaged courses of at least three months, and up to two years, which would be recognised by the Council as post-qualification studies.

The Birch Report gave significant support to these proposals and stressed 'the importance of employers finding ways in which staff can be released to undertake the additional study and supervised practice' (DHSS 1976, p. 93). 'For staff with a basic qualification, extended further training (as opposed to short courses) is in our view essential to the development of adequate specialist expertise in the various fields of work of the personal social services including that of management' (DHSS 1976, p. 127). To achieve this, the report set out ambitious targets for post-qualification training. The two key recommendations were that all CSS and CQSW holders should have the equivalent of three months post-qualifying training every five years, and that 10 per cent of CQSW holders should have a substantial period of post-qualifying training, at least to the equivalent of twelve months, at some point in their career.

Even with no expansion of total numbers of those undertaking the CSS and CQSW qualifying training, the targets required a twelvefold expansion of the resources devoted to qualifying training. Unhappily the growth envisaged by Birch did not materialise. There were a number of post-qualifying programmes developed, but the total number of places available was limited – and even that proved an overestimate of the potential market from local authorities, for many of the programmes experienced difficulty in filling all the places available.

Now the thrust from CCETSW is to develop DSW and the lower level of qualification. Its policy is clear. 'Council hopes that as soon as possible after the (Q)DSW is established it will provide the foundation for post-experience/qualification training. . . . Council believes it essential that funding of the basic qualifying social work programme should be established first' (CCETSW 1987a, p. 31). There is unlikely therefore to be significant further progress in a network of post-qualification training before the end of the century.

It is ironic that the most significant development in post-qualification training should have come not as a result of a

CCETSW initiative, but of legislative pressure. The requirement in the Mental Health Act 1983 (and later but comparable legislation in Scotland and Northern Ireland) that local authorities should appoint approved social workers to undertake certain functions under the legislation, and that would be contingent on the social worker having successfully completed a period of training as directed by the Secretary of State, has imposed on local authorities a requirement to plan a substantial period of specialist post-qualification study for a group of staff.

The aim of the legislation was to improve the standard of practice in work with mentally ill people. The dispute with NALGO about the use of a written examination, and the validity of a pass/fail judgement being applied should not obscure the importance of the legislative recognition that the basic qualification was inadequate in itself to safeguard the rights of clients. There is now within social services departments a growing cadre of staff with specialist knowledge and skills in working with a client group which have been tested against an externally determined standard. This model lends itself to replication in other areas of specialist practice. Child-abuse work is one obvious example, where additional training could serve a wider political purpose by defusing some of the current anxieties about practice competence in this area.

Has Training Improved the Quality of Practice?

To ask this question is rather like asking about the emperor's new clothes. Implicit in what has been written above, in numerous Government statements, public inquiries, CCETSW papers, employer attitudes and trade union policies is the assumption that training and improved standards of practice go together. That should be the case, but it would be wrong to ignore the existence of dissenting voices. It would also be wrong to ignore the fact that the grounds for criticism have shifted over time. The main areas of attack have been the preoccupation with casework, the lack of fit between training and practice, the misplaced emphasis on social work rather than social care, the individualist perspective of training and practice, and the failure to develop skills in working with other disciplines and professions as a Fortress Social Services mentality has developed.

Social work has been criticised as being exclusively concerned with a poor man's psychotherapy – casework – as its method of intervention. It is true that the emphasis in training during the sixties was heavily placed on casework. The theories of human growth and development which underpinned training borrowed heavily from psychiatry. But beyond the high priests of the Tavistock Clinic, and those working in child-guidance settings, there is little practical evidence of widespread use of quasi-therapeutic methods of intervention. The Biestek principles (1961) have been substantially modified under the dominant influence of agency setting. Perhaps a balanced view is that social casework is one of a range of means of intervention in social situations. Many would argue that workload pressures within social services are such that there is no time and space for the leisurely casework process.

Of more substance is the contention that the present pattern of training has little relevance to practice. This has been argued by some Directors of Social Services alarmed by the radicalised products of some courses, and by the amount of on-the-job learning required by newly-qualified social workers. The expressed desire of employers for more control over curriculum content was met within the CSS structure, and the model of collaborative planning for DSW courses draws heavily on the partnership model developed in CSS. While educational programmes need to be relevant to the work setting, a questioning critical spirit should be developed during training. It would be tragic if the defensiveness of thin-skinned Directors of Social Services were allowed to interfere with academic enquiry. More valid as a criticism is the unpreparedness of some students for the work setting. Two main reasons for this are evident. First, too many students have been allowed to pass being given the benefit of every possible doubt (Davies and Brandon 1979) by pusillanimous tutors and practice teachers. Second, there is a genuine problem in covering in adequate detail the full range of personal social services responsibilities in a two-year course.

The emphasis in social work training is still predominantly placed on helping individuals and families with the problems which they are experiencing in personal relationships within the family or in their interactions with the environment. This has been a persistent source of criticism. It has several effects which operate to the detriment of effective intervention. First, it tends to lead to problems being viewed in isolation from the network of family and community supports potentially available. The Barclay Report drew attention to this, suggesting a greater need for 'social care planning'. Secondly, it militates against effective management and social policy planning by regarding each social problem as unique, thus making social workers suspicious of aggregating groups of cases to identify trends. Thirdly, it emphasises individual and family pathology rather than structural factors, again diminishing the 'political' component of social work. And fourthly, its emphasis on the case means that too little attention is given to the possibility of developing work with groups, or to work with wider communities. This is particularly unfortunate in residential and day care settings where there are opportunities to take positive advantage of group care. The unitary approach attempts to address these criticisms, but there remains a real difficulty in translating broader societal perspectives into agency referral and allocation procedures.

The imbalance between social work and social care is closely argued by Webb and Wistow (1987, pp. 212–33). Unlike the tarnished image of field social work, the social care services are regarded as providing direct practical assistance to individuals in need. Webb and Wistow argue that the thrust of professionalisation, and training resources, have gone disproportionately to the former. As noted above, the proposed allocation of resources between DSW and CSC suggests that this imbalance will be perpetuated.

The growth of social services bureaucracies, and the fortress mentality inculcated by press criticism, have created an inward-looking service, reluctant to push out the frontiers of intervention. This is a reaction against being seen as 'universal providers', but means that social services have not been active in boundary areas like general practice, social security offices and schools where their counselling role could make a real impact. As a consequence, skills in working with other disciplines have been relatively neglected in qualifying training. When some of the most exciting initiatives are taking place in the context of multi-disciplinary teams like Community Mental Handicap Teams and Community Mental Health Centres, this is a disappointing omission. There have been some initiatives in developing joint training with mental handicap nurses, particularly in Wales where the All-Wales Strategy for Mental Handicap is producing more open attitudes to breaking down professional barriers, but this stands out as the exception in the overall picture.

The concepts developed in the Griffiths report of case management will pose new problems for trainers. The skills required of brokerage, negotiation, contract specification and budgeting are not the stuff of qualifying training courses at present but if the case manager concept – discussed more fully in Chapter 6 – is widely adopted, it will be essential to provide opportunities for staff to develop these skills.

There is then some substance in the array of criticisms levelled against qualifying training. It would be surprising if it were otherwise. No training in any field can constitute a complete preparation for practice. No training can reflect all the divergent strands of opinion, fad and fancy within social work, and no training can provide a wholly comprehensive introduction to legal, practice and administrative aspects of work in a variety of settings. But while acknowledging this, one is left with the basic challenge whether the increased proportion of trained staff has been reflected in improved quality of service to the client.

The evidence on improved standards of service is at best ambiguous. There are consistent reports demonstrating a relatively high level of customer satisfaction with the services received, but many of these services are practically orientated, with little input from trained and qualified staff. Whether recipients of social work services would share this favourable view is less certain although one must recognise the public sector characteristic that critics of services have ready access to the media in the way denied – or unsought by – satisfied users.

But customer satisfaction, while apposite to the marketplace, is a crude indicator of quality in personal social services. True, it is important that services are perceived as accessible, responsive, flexible and – in computerspeak – user-friendly. But services can meet all those tests, but still fail on the test of effectiveness. In the discussion of the three E's in Chapter 5, questions are raised about the effectiveness of intervention. The vagueness of objectives contributes to the methodological problems of discussing effectiveness.

Social work does give comfort to people in distress. It does provide support to those oppressed by problems and difficulties. It represents a point of contact with public services that should be human, friendly and sensitive to the particular needs of individuals and families. Arguably, that is sufficient justification for the role that it occupies in the network of community provision. The willingness of public services to reach out in an undemanding way to support social casualties is an important value statement about our society. But it is social work itself which would regard this as inadequate as a justification, for its expansion has been predicated on its ability to change, and by implication improve the attitudes and behaviour of these social casualties. The social control functions, often rejected by social workers on political and professional grounds, are in reality fundamental. It is not philanthropy which dictates the allocation of resources to personal social services, but a public recognition that the homeless, the mentally disordered, the isolated elderly, mentally handicapped people and fractured families constitute a threat to the stability of family and social structures. Public resources can legitimately be employed to shore up these structures, and social work with its ability to strengthen personal and social functioning is the chosen instrument. Social support – the maintenance function – is part of that process. Personal change and development is the traditional *raison d'être* of social work intervention, but the creation of social services departments has made it possible to see that aspect of the work as one part – and a fairly small part – of the network of personal social services.

Haltingly, services are moving towards greater effectiveness with clarity about objectives, about the target population and about the means of delivery. It is wrong to judge personal social services as a whole by social work, and wrong to judge the impact of training in terms exclusively of social work intervention. The case for training may still be unproven but overall the combination of improved management, better organisational structures, and higher levels of training has addressed some of the confusion rampant in the mid-seventies. The relationship between social work as a profession and the personal social services as a whole is considered further in Chapter 8.

5

Organisation and Structure

It is remarkable that the present organisational structure for the delivery of social welfare provision, including social work, was devised over twenty years ago in the Seebohm Report. Given the changes in the social and professional environment which have taken place in that time, it is unsurprising that the continued validity of that structure is now subject to more critical scrutiny than at any time since the Report was published.

Before looking at the strengths and weaknesses of the structure recommended by Seebohm – a large local authority department drawing together formerly specialised services and able to command substantial resources – it is helpful briefly to consider the options discarded by the Committee. These were:

(a) Undertaking further research and experiment before a decision. This was rightly rejected as unjustifiable procrastination.

(b) The existing structure to be retained with more formalised machinery for coordination. While attractive in terms of minimal disruption, this was rejected because of the inherent problems of a coordinating committee without executive powers, and its lack of impact on fieldwork practice.

(c) Two departments – one for children and families, and one for the elderly and handicapped. This was rejected as perpetuating a symptom-centred approach to family difficulties, preventing treatment of the family as a whole and impairing continuity of care.

(d) A social casework department acting on an agency basis for other departments. This was rejected as splitting social work artificially from service provision.

(e) Absorption into enlarged health departments. This was rejected as impractical, and as failing to provide the required focus on social care needs.
(f) Removal of social services from local government. This was rejected as failing to give due weight to citizen participation and close links with the community.

It will be realised at once that there is a strongly contemporary flavour to these options. The question is whether in the light of experience, the judgement reached in the Seebohm Report remains valid. To decide that, one must first look at how effective the organisational structure has proved in meeting the objectives set.

As is evident from the options discarded by Seebohm, the location of personal social services in local government was not a forgone conclusion. The probation service is an example of a centrally-funded, locally-administered social work service outside the ambit of public accountability, at least in the sense of locally-elected members exercising control. Its ability to secure resources compares favourably with the performance of most social services departments. Its insulation from the vagaries of political accountability has at times been the envy of social services colleagues in England and Wales. Yet in Scotland, probation is a local government service delivered by local authority social workers without evident detriment to the quality of service. There is therefore no reason inherent in the nature of the service which determines organisational location. Tradition may often be a more powerful argument than rationality in determining such matters, and the location of children's, welfare and mental health services in local government at the time of Seebohm's deliberations was a powerful argument for the *status quo*.

Drawing fragmented services into a closer unity was a predictable outcome of the Seebohm Committee's deliberations. Hall (1976) has provided a fascinating account of the way in which the Committee worked, and how it reached its conclusions. The aim of the recommendations was a department which would command more resources, achieve better coordination, improve client access to services, create a professional career structure, work closely with the community, and extend concepts of social planning to other local authority departments. While social services departments have been criticised for their bureaucracy, insensitivity and unresponsiveness, these major objectives of reorganisation were mainly secured after an initially traumatic period of organisational chaos.

Social services departments did command resources and grew faster than any other local authority service. They did achieve a coordination of service inputs, although there remain difficulties even within a single department in securing full integration of fieldwork, day care, domiciliary and residential services. Client access was improved and a new emphasis given to work with families. The advantages of that stability were somewhat vitiated by the success in creating a career structure as the rapidity of growth created promotional opportunities, and thus led to a very rapid turnover of staff in the early and mid-seventies. Less success has been enjoyed in bringing services closer to the community, and it is doubtful how far social services have influenced corporate thinking in most local authorities.

The balance-sheet in terms of objectives is thus heavily weighted in favour of the credit side. The reorganisation became the envy of many European countries where welfare provision continued to display the characteristics of fragmentation and poor coordination, and where the professional social worker was often subordinate to the administrator. And 'the very diversity which makes the SSD's difficult to describe in simple terms ensures an ability to put together different packages of help for different client groups' (Webb and Wistow 1987, p. 50).

The placing of this new large department in local government had immediate implications for status. Children's Officers and Welfare Officers had been second-rank chief officers on a par with the Chief Librarian in contrast to the powerful figures heading Housing, Education and Legal Services. Now in one bound, social welfare moved to the top table and to a more senior position at that table. And as Chief Officers at the head of a service, Directors built a pyramid structure beneath them through which to organise, manage and control service delivery. Small personal departments were converted almost overnight into large megaliths with a lack of clarity about roles and responsibilities. Directors themselves were regarded as remote figures divorced from an awareness of the realities of practice.

In the setting-up period for social services departments, the work undertaken at Brunel based upon Jacques' theory of the 'span of discretion' was extremely influential (Kogan and Terry 1971; Rowbottom, Hey and Billis 1974). It identified a number of hierarchical levels within the organisation. No real consideration was given to alternative models. Concepts like the career social worker operating, as consultants do in a hospital context, as independent practitioners with command over resources, or the welfare unit with practitioner influence paramount, never moved beyond the written page into practice. The size and scale of the enterprise in its local government context demanded hierarchy. And if social services were, as Seebohm hoped, to exercise influence on other local authority departments like planning, education and housing, it was necessary to play the game by the prescribed rules. An alternative approach but still within a hierarchical framework would have been a far more decentralised, polyarchic structure with delegation of resource allocation and decision-making to area offices and residential units. It was to be another decade before the Barclay Report was to recommend such an approach (Barclay 1982, p. 129).

Changing Approaches to Structures

Having determined to accept a hierarchical model of organisation, authorities then had to choose whether to divide responsibilities on functional – residential, fieldwork, day and domiciliary – geographic, or client group lines. The latter option was discarded straightaway. It smacked too much of the specialist services preceding reorganisation instead of the new beginning sought. The majority of departments chose a functional division of responsibilities, but years of experience and innumerable restructurings have brought a change in emphasis. It should be noted that the kneejerk local authority response to organisational problems is to change structure, a response which usually achieves the unhappy trinity of failing to identify the problems properly, producing a change which fails to address the problems, and thus adding further problems to those originally presented. People, not structures, make organisations work. Yet there are trends that one can see in the changes which have taken place in structures and they reflect shifts in social and professional attitudes.

First, there has been a shift away from functional management.
The notion of dividing responsibilities by setting has been over-
taken by the emergence of a more flexible pattern of service
provision. Fieldworkers are no longer involved only in assessing
the need for other forms of provision, but actively engaged in
some of the work undertaken in day care and residential settings.
Day centres are no longer isolated from the mainstream of care,
and residential homes occupy a wider role in services offering
short-term care, day care and sometimes a range of other services
to the client group. The importance of easy and clear communication between the settings has been increasingly recognised, as in
their contact with social services agencies, clients are likely to use a
number of different services. That communication is facilitated
when there are no artificial management lines dividing services.

Secondly, there has been a reassertion of the value of specialisation, although the specialisations are not necessarily those of
the former separate departments. Intake work, child abuse, work
with the under-fives, homefinding teams, are all new specialisations – by no means found in all departments – but having to be
accommodated within organisational structures. In organisational
terms, it is specialisation by client group which has been the most
powerful influence on structures. Five broad client groups can be
identified – children's services, those for mentally handicapped
people, mental health services, services to elderly people and
services to those with physical disabilities. Increasingly one finds
organisational structures incorporating client group responsibility
at senior management level.

Thirdly – and in conflict with the reassertion of specialisation –
there has been a renewed awareness of the significance of geography. The Seebohm vision of close links with the local community
was reasserted in the Barclay Report on the role and tasks of social
workers. While Barclay stressed that community social work was
not exclusively linked to locality, and suggested that it could
extend to community of interest – for instance, families with a
mentally handicapped relative – the primary emphasis in the
Report itself was on community social work based on locality. The
three examples cited were resource centres in residential establishments, outposting of social workers to health centres and schools,
and the development of patch teams.

The concept of patch teams has been most clearly articulated by

Hadley and McGrath (1984). It involves first the organisation of statutory services at a local level, defined by Hadley and others as 'street or village level' (Barclay 1982, p. 227) involving 'a readily recognisable contact person in every neighbourhood, whether a home help, ancillary or even a volunteer who has direct links with the local office'. Secondly, the integration of domiciliary services with social work service, and particularly with informal caring networks, is essential to ensure a proper mix of statutory and informal provision. Thirdly, there is a blurring of roles between neighbourhood workers, domiciliary staff and social workers. Fourthly, local teams require substantial delegation of both resources and decision-making to be sufficiently responsive to clients and neighbourhoods.

The implications of patch approaches for practice were considered in Chapter 2. It is sufficient here to note that the move to locally-based service provision has had a potent appeal. It has been presented as a means of effectively utilising informal caring networks, and of breaking down the professional mystique. As a vehicle for low-cost solutions to social problems, this has made it attractive to some Tory local authorities. East Sussex has gone further than most in transforming its pattern of service delivery. But patch has also had a powerful appeal to the Left, which has welcomed the neighbourhood office as a base for housing, social services and advice provision as a means of improving access and visibility.

Some form of decentralisation has been developed in up to a third of social services authorities (Murray 1987), but the phrase covers many different concepts. For some it is the means to develop community control of services supplementing the political process; for others it is a reflection of trends in society favouring smaller units.

Where local authorities have decentralised their service delivery, this has been reflected in their organisational structure. The central bureaucracies have been markedly reduced with a slimming-down of senior management. Non-operational senior posts have proved particularly vulnerable at times of reorganisation. Administration, training, planning and research have tended to be relegated from senior management positions. In the early years of social services, the pace of capital development meant that planning was a vital component of senior management decision-making. Now the task is one of redeploying existing resources rather than one of commissioning new buildings, and this has been reflected in the diminution of the planning role.

The Impact of Joint Planning of Community Care

As planning has diminished in significance, it has been replaced by the requirement for joint planning of health and personal social services. The introduction of joint planning in 1974 and the lubricant of joint finance are discussed in Chapter 6. What needs to be noted here is that the increasing involvement with the Health Service was not reflected in managerial arrangements. Despite the recommendation of the Working Party on Collaboration for the specific appointment of a Senior Officer with particular responsibility for developing liaison between the health authority and social services, such a role tended to be treated as an additional task for an Assistant Director rather than justifying a separate post. The impetus for community care therefore came from finance and not from managerial commitment. As authorities were squeezed for revenue funds, they came to use joint finance primarily as an additional supplement for revenue developments. With the advent of financial penalties on those authorities deemed to be high-spending, introduced by the Conservative Government in 1980, there has been a further switch of emphasis with health authorities utilising a growing share of joint finance – currently around 20 per cent of available funds – for their own schemes to develop community services.

Community care has become the catalyst for change in organisational structures. It has been government policy since the late 1950s to reduce the numbers of people housed in long-stay institutions. A series of Government documents (DHSS 1971; DHSS 1975; DHSS 1981; DHSS 1981b) have set down policy objectives based on developing for the main client-groups a programme of community provision. Ten years' experience of joint planning has shown that even with the assistance of joint finance, progress towards that policy objective has been disappointingly slow. Both the House of Commons Select Committee on Social Services and the Audit Commission have analysed the reasons for the slow rate of progress (1985, 1986). As a consequence Sir Roy Griffiths was asked to review the options for change in organisational and financial structures.

The Audit Commission's analysis has been widely praised. While recognising that some progress had been made, it noted that in some areas the number of residential and day care places newly available was lagging behind the rundown of long-stay institutions. The unevenness of local authority provision also militated against any comprehensive strategy, with over half the authorities spending less than £1 per head of population on mental health services. But the Commission discounted the need for more resources as the primary issue facing community care services, and identified seven structural problems which needed to be addressed:

1 *Funding mechanisms* At a time when explicit policies required the shift of resources from hospital-based services to the community, expenditure on NHS mental illness and mental handicap inpatient services increased in real terms by 100 million pounds between 1976 and 1984.

2 *Local authority finance* The grant system can operate to penalise local authorities wishing to build up community services. The system of targets and penalties introduced in 1980 was superseded by ratecapping, but neither made any differentiation between spending to achieve Government policy objectives and other forms of spending.

3 *Limited bridging finance* Only 100 million a year of total NHS spending in excess of 3 billion is available for joint finance or the dowry mechanisms introduced in 1982.

4 *Supplementary benefit policies* The ready availability of social security funding to support private residential care contrasts with the absence of a private sector in day and domiciliary care. The rapid expansion of private care means that the total number of elderly people in all residential settings has increased from 207 700 in 1974 to 269 300 in 1984, a rate of increase far greater than the increase in the total elderly population.

5 *Inequities in distribution* Despite the efforts of Government through RAWP (the basis of regional distribution of health care finance which takes its acronym from the Resource Allocation Working Party which devised it) and Rate Support Grant to ensure a fair distribution, the effects are largely offset by Supplementary Benefit payments for board and lodging. Such

payments are not targeted on the basis of need, and are very
unevenly distributed. There are nearly ten times as many places in
private and voluntary homes in Devon as there are in Cleveland –
a reflection of relative attractiveness to potential users rather than
differential need.

6 *Fragmentation* Responsibility for the introduction of community
care involves services from a variety of agencies, voluntary groups
and the informal care network provided by family and friends.
Developing effective packages for people in care therefore requires a heavy input of time in planning and coordination. Some
indication of the political complexity may be seen in Figure 5.1.

7 *Staffing arrangements* Sound manpower planning and effective
training are absent in relation to community care. The Audit
Commission noted a more rapid increase in the numbers of mental
handicap hospital nurses than in community nurses over the ten-
year period from 1974 to 1984.

This analysis constituted a far more thoroughgoing critique of
Government policy on community care than had previously been
undertaken. Incremental improvements to health and social services structures can be traced from the initial joint planning
circular in 1974, the introduction of joint finance and the 1981
Consultative document *Care in the Community* (DHSS 1981).
With the Audit Commission report, and the overall review of
primary health care initiated by the Green Paper on Primary
Health Care and the Cumberlege Report on neighbourhood
nursing, the debate shifted. The discussion was no longer how to
operate existing structures more effectively but had shifted to
consider how structures needed to be amended to achieve
governmental objectives.

Without minimising the scale of the shift in attitudes, there is a
continuity of thinking in the ideas under consideration which can
be traced back to the 1981 Consultative Document, *Care in the
Community*. They were at that time rejected, but their reappear-
ance demands a critical analysis of the implications for social work
practice of any organisational changes envisaged. Social work will
have a key role in the implementation of any changes because it
has acquired unique skills and experience in coordination and
devising individualised programmes. Whatever the organisational
structure, social workers will be required to respond to need, and

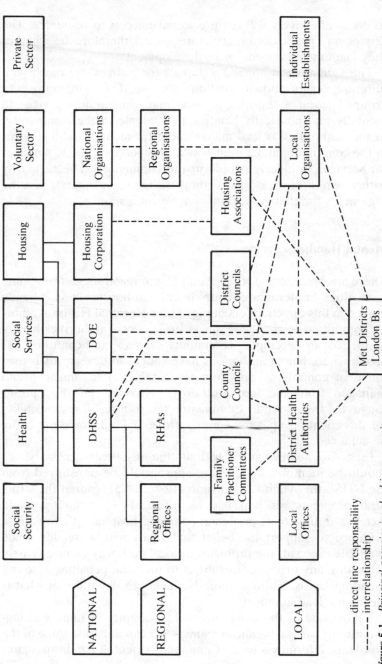

Figure 5.1 *Principal agencies involved in community care*

to do so effectively will require to have access to resources. The test of any proposals on structure should therefore be whether they facilitate or impede these developments.

The Commission applied a 'horses for courses' approach with different organisational solutions for the three long-term care groups – local authorities as lead management for services to mentally and physically handicapped people in the community, health authorities as lead management for mental health services in the community and a joint board to supervise a single manager for services to elderly people in the community. The regularity with which these ideas of structural change recur suggests that the arguments for change warrant some examination.

Mental Handicap Services

There are precedents for the Audit Commission suggestion. Some authorities conterminous with health authorities have already moved in this direction, encouraged by a Regional Health Authority committed to change (Francis 1987). Local authorities have a major role in developing community services, and confusion has arisen where health authorities have sought to develop their own range of community provision separately staffed, financed and managed from the local authority provision. Of the options canvassed by the Audit Commission the transfer of responsibility for this client group is the least controversial but would not easily be achieved.

In saying somewhat glibly that 'the resources necessary . . . should be identified and, where appropriate be transferred from the NHS', the Audit Commission (1986, p. 75) ignored the structural problems which it had identified. First, given the rapid increase in unit costs in mental handicap hospitals, there is little evidence to support the belief that funds will be readily made available. Second, the problems of local authority finance remain acute in many urban areas subject to financial penalties as 'overspending' areas. Thirdly, there has been no definition of what is meant by 'lead authority'.

Taking one of the more successful examples of joint working-community mental handicap teams – one can illustrate some of the problems left unresolved. Community mental handicap teams draw together workers from different disciplines – social workers, nurses, paramedical staff, psychologists, psychiatrists and GPs. Operational policies for the teams vary from the 'integrated' with a single team manager, who has managerial authority over individual team members, to the 'polyarchic' where members agree on a coordinator, but each team member is managerially and professionally accountable to a line manager within their respective discipline. The tensions inherent in this situation have led some teams to shed their professional allegiances altogether, with social workers, nurses and psychologists serving as team members wholly accountable to the team manager and in practice submerging their professional identity in the wider unit.

It is difficult to visualise how community mental handicap teams could operate with social services as lead authority without such readiness to merge professional backgrounds. Whether this will be acceptable to all disciplines is an open question.

One striking example of success can be seen in the All-Wales strategy. As in Scotland and Northern Ireland, the arm of central government – the Welsh Office – has the opportunity to switch money between budget heads and thus create some flexibility in the system. Considerable sums have been used to 'bridge' by investing in community services prior to running down the scale of in-patient provision (Welsh Office 1983). The key element in the development of services has been flexibility and a readiness to adapt services to meet individual needs. These characteristics, rather than structural change, may be the best way of achieving progress.

Mental Health Services

The very title of this section touches upon a crucial conceptual gap between health and social services attitudes. From a health care perspective people are seen in terms of diagnosis treatment and prognosis. Sick people with illnesses are treated, and sometimes cured. From a social services perspective, mental health is seen as part of a spectrum from wellbeing to psychosis with an individual's position on the spectrum, dependent on a mix of social, environmental and dietary factors as well as the psychiatric condition of the individual. This argument is further developed in Chapter 7 when the tensions between health and social services views are explored in detail.

The role of the lead authority envisages health as the major provider of services, but falling short of total management responsibility for all services. Local authorities would continue to offer services, but health authorities would contract with local authorities to buy in their services. This would entail an agreement to finance a given number of day centre places, an allocation of home-help time, social work support, and so on. One immediate problem can be seen in this brave new world. Given human fallibility, what happens if a wrong estimate has been made of the places required or hours support to be funded? Services cannot be turned on and off like a tap, and there may well be blockages in the supply system.

One has again to refer back to the Commission's structural analysis. If local authorities are subject to a manpower ceiling, a freeze on filling vacancies to contain spending, or a real and imminent fear of financial penalties, they are unlikely to respond to the blandishments of the health authority to expand services with no long-term commitment. As the contracts made by the lead authority with providers of services would be like those of General Managers and time-limited, there would be little incentive for local authorities to make the provision sought.

It is interesting to test out the model of good practice described in the Commission's report against its own organisational solution. Torbay has developed a service around community mental health centres, which serve as the focus for mental health services in the district. Table 5.1 shows the residential provision for mentally-ill people.

The model service has shifted the balance of care towards the community. This plan was produced jointly by social services and health. How would it have differed if health only had been involved, and would it have eased the process? The answers can only be speculative, but there are some unvarying truths. First, social services have long-established arrangements negotiated locally with housing departments and housing associations to provide special-needs housing. For most health authorities, this is new territory and therefore time-consuming learning will be necessary. Secondly, local authorities could be in a competitive situation for the best sites if they are to be the lead authority for

Table 5.1 *Services for mentally ill people: residential settings (example: Torbay serving 225 000)*

Providing agency	Form of care	Service
District housing Private sector	Unstaffed group homes with support	25 ordinary houses supported by domiciliary and day care provision
Voluntary sector	Voluntary sector group homes	4 group homes run by MIND
District housing Social Services Private sector	Sheltered lodgings	Normal housing with landladies or 'adult fostering'
District housing Housing association	Core and cluster scheme	3 or 4 houses supported by warden/general manager and domiciliary services
District housing Private housing Health and social services staff	Staffed group homes	4 houses for 4 or 5 people each with residential staff support
Private sector	Residential homes	Mainly for the older age range
Health authority	Health service hostels	3 hostels
Health authority	Hospital	60 beds (acute short-term)

Source: *Mental Illness: A Strategy for the Future* (South Devon Social Services, Devon County Council).

provision for mentally handicapped people. Thirdly, local authorities will continue as the registration authority for private residential homes, and criteria for registration would have to be the subject of joint discussion between health and social services. Fourthly, the bulk of residential provision with the exception of unstaffed group homes would fall under the managerial ambit of the lead authority. It is questionable whether the skills are yet developed among health professionals to operate a loose-fit, flexible structure differing in ethos so radically from hospital provision. In summary, there may be few advantages with many disbenefits from the proposed reallocation of responsibility.

When one looks at domiciliary services and day care, the difficulties mentioned above in terms of prediction recur. The end-result could well be a loss of flexibility, with a structure that looks neat on paper but which gets in the way of a flexible, individually-tailored package of care for the mentally ill person.

A subsidiary option mentioned by the Commission for mental health services was the joint board approach. The advantages and disadvantages of this are illustrated in the context of the elderly, for whom it is suggested as the appropriate organisational solution.

Elderly People

The proposal for a joint board with representatives from both health and social services may be less significant as a precursor of future patterns than the way in which the Audit Commission suggested that the Board should discharge its responsibilities. This was through a single manager with a single budget, able to purchase, from whichever public or private agency seems appropriate, services for elderly people in the area for which he or she is responsible'. The concept was endorsed by Griffiths but located in his proposals for local authorities acting through a 'case manager' where significant resources were involved.

The most striking feature of the proposal is the ideology of the market which underpins the concept. This owes much to the concept of buying in packages of care which was presented in the Kent Community Care Project (Davies and Challis 1986). Social workers were given direct control of a budget limited to an expenditure per case of two-thirds of the cost of a place in a residential home. They were expected to undertake more extensive social work activity with elderly people and their families, to focus on neighbourhood resources and to stimulate options like boarding-out. The study found a lower rate of entry to residential care and lower use of long-term hospital care facilities, and a greater cost-effectiveness compared with a group with identical characteristics receiving the usual pattern of service. In particular, the study found a closer correlation between dependency and the level of service offered than was true of those receiving a regular service. The workers showed a greater sensitivity to the potential of informal care.

Westland has offered a robust critique of this approach writ large as envisaged by its adoption as the mainspring of managing community care. He envisages the local manager using a budget supplied by health and social services authorities to buy services from the same authorities, and questions whether there is a 'reserve pool of unemployed home helps, domiciliary and day care workers, social workers and others who could spring into action and into paid employment' if required by the local manager (Westland 1987). In practice it is more likely that paid staff from the parent authorities would be seconded to the manager. In practice the Griffiths model of locating the case manager squarely within an existing statutory agency serves to overcome some of the difficulties, for the case manager would call upon existing resources to create a package of care.

Objections to Change

Some of the problems associated with the structural changes proposed have been identified in the consideration of the Audit Commission options. But there are fundamental objections which need to be noted. Paramount among these is the implied retreat from direct political accountability with a further limitation of local government control. This may be consistent with the thrust of Government policy, but it is arguable that local democracy has a responsiveness to local needs not always evident in health care provision and structures. Whether the informed consumer can replace the elected representative in ensuring that services are responsive to local users is still an open question.

Secondly, structural changes do not address the issues of coterminosity of boundaries between health and local authorities which bedevil effective cooperation at present at local level. Structural change brings in its wake organisational problems. Before embarking on change, one needs first to be confident that the benefits outweigh the substantial disruption which is inevitably associated with major organisational shifts.

Implications for Social Work

The debate currently taking place about the future shape of services has implications for practice, particularly because certain common elements are discernible in what is viewed as a 'good' service by the parties involved. The Audit Commission noted some characteristics of successful initiatives in community care, and these are echoed by the studies carried out by the Personal Social Services Research Unit on the pilot projects funded as part of the Care in the Community programme.

The Audit Commission suggested six characteristics:

1 *Strong and committed local champions of change* In each successful scheme there were one or two people determined to overcome obstacles and to establish good working relationships with colleagues in other disciplines. Unhappily, one cannot guarantee such individuals in each area.

2 *Focus on action, not bureaucratic machinery* Teams focused on achieving a specific project within agreed time-scales and budgets were noticeably more successful than those of joint groups with a loose, ill-defined remit.

3 *Locally integrated services* These were found where links of geography and responsibility facilitated linkages between social services and health authority managers, and where mutual trust had been established.

4 *Focus on the local neighbourhood* The use of informal care and identification of community resources were evident in the successful community care schemes.

5 *Team approach* The development of community handicap teams, community mental handicap teams, and primary care teams produced a situation where the sum of resources was greater than the constituent parts working individually.

6 *Partnership between statutory and voluntary organisations* Voluntary organisations like Homestart and Crossroads provided flexible and cost-effective services in line with the overall strategic objectives of the statutory services.

The report notes acidly that these characteristics 'amount to a radical departure from the generally accepted ways of doing things at present' (Audit Commission 1986, p. 73). That may be an unduly harsh comment, for social services throughout the 1980s have been attempting to move towards these characteristics. The focus on the neighbourhood, the importance of teamworking and the need to take a broad view of social care planning were all clearly stated in the Barclay Report (Barclay 1982) in its view of community social work. The controversy which followed the publication of the report may have distorted the degree of consensus which existed about the desirability of moving in that direction.

To Pinker, social work is based on social casework incorporating counselling and various practical tasks. To Hadley and colleagues, a broader view is appropriate with a reduced emphasis on counselling and a greater emphasis on indirect work through lay people, melting the barriers between professional and non-professional aspects of social work. To the Central Council for Education and Training in Social Work, a broader view of social work was also deemed appropriate

> in the sense that social work skill and expertise are increasingly used in a wider range of situations and posts than used to be the case. . . . Other services, both voluntary and statutory, are increasingly seeing social work knowledge and expertise as underpinning the whole service, even though all staff working with clients do not need to be qualified as social workers (CCETSW 1985).

Two elements need clarification. First, social work is sometimes being used interchangeably with social services. While these departments are the primary employers, they are by no means the only employers of social workers, who may be found in private and voluntary organisations as well as other public sector bodies. Secondly, social work and social care are being confused with a lack of clear definition of the specific social work task. These two confusions recur in relation to both practice and training.

It is particularly important to see social work as a separate discipline which at present is practised predominantly in the setting of social services and social work departments, in view of the likelihood that a far more diversified pattern of employment will emerge in the next few years. A more plural system of welfare provision would have the effect of forcing a rethinking of current roles and a focus on what truly constitutes the distinctive contribution of social work's knowledge and skills in new organisational frameworks.

Some tentative conclusions can be drawn from the current

debate about structures – a debate which is in part political, in part philosophical, and in part practical.

Political trends

There is a fundamental hostility to local government in the policies and attitudes of the Government. Fuelled by what it sees as the abuse of local authority powers in pursuit of overtly political objectives, albeit by a minority of authorities, the Government is pushing forward with a range of centralising measures which reduce the room for manoeuvre of local political leadership. The combination of media hostility and an ideological climate hostile to public sector bureaucracies has created a political environment in which change to long-established social services structures is not only possible, but probable.

The salience of health service issues in political debate has continued with an unparalleled debate about the financial needs of health care and how they can best be met. Direct ministerial involvement in the running of the Health Service with Ministers chairing both the Supervisory and Management Boards will ensure that health care issues continue to have high political priority. The direction of change which is eventually adopted may well have implications for welfare provision, for many of the options now under discussion in the health care context are potentially applicable to social services, from the internal market to private care funded through insurance.

Philosophical trends

A belief in a plural system of welfare has been consistently articulated by Ministers. Hitherto there has been little substance to the rhetoric with minimal change to the structure of statutory services, with the lone exception of the emergence of a flourishing private care sector in residential care, which has major implications for the regulatory role of the public sector. Similarly the health service has not been challenged as the best means of delivering the majority of health care, while the private sector has continued to expand in a climate of benevolent neutrality. Parker and Etherington have drawn attention to the consistency within Government policy with public sector housing being sold off to sitting tenants, housing associations or cooperatives, or private developers, with the goal of breaking up the monopoly position of the local authority in the provision of rented accommodation. In education the extension of parental choice and parental participation is presented as a counterbalancing force to the public sector monopoly power with schools being able to opt out of the local authority sector. Parker and Etherington suggest that personal social services will be next in line with the breakup of monopoly provision and the extension of consumer choice as the justification presented for these changes (Parker and Etherington 1987).

The voucher concept which has been considered and discarded for the last twenty-five years is again being dusted down and packaged as a means of enhancing consumer power without destroying the fabric of current services. When such ideas are seriously discussed one begins to realise the degree to which thinking on social policy has been 'monetarised', with every aspect viewed predominantly in terms of the cost of provision and the market seen as the best regulator in all areas of life. Consumer choice is seen as the justification for these changes with a plural system not only cheaper but better in its responsiveness to consumer needs expressed through the market.

The case manager approach involves professionals making choices on behalf of consumers about the best mix of services to meet the needs of the client. How far this meets the aspiration of promoting consumer choice is questionable, unless the greater freedom of the case manager to 'buy in' services results in the advent of a number of small providers from whom the individual client can choose.

The debate about welfare pluralism is still fairly undeveloped because it has been caught in a wider argument about public policy in the provision of welfare. There are two strands to Government thinking which need to be considered separately. First there is seen to be a benefit from the development of a range of suppliers of services both to the user in terms of maximising choice but also to the State in terms of the discipline on costs injected by competition among service providers. Secondly, there is the view that private and voluntary provision is inherently better and that the role of public provision should accordingly be diminished.

It has to be recognised that the market introduces an element of uncertainty into the planning and development of services. Thus

the development of private residential care for the elderly sub-
sidised by social security finance has had the effect of sharply
increasing the numbers of elderly people in institutional settings,
directly counter to the stated thrust of public policy to support
elderly people in their own homes. There is as yet little evidence of
real competition emerging because the market is distorted by the
subsidy available from social security; nor is there any evidence to
suggest that informed choices are being made about the different
homes available in a locality. Despite the finding in the research
undertaken for the Firth Report (Bradshaw and Gibbs 1988) that
only 7 per cent of admissions were inappropriate – a startling
contrast to the Audit Commission view that up to a third of
admissions were unnecessary – the suspicion lingers that the profit
motive may have led to a widening of the eligibility criteria and
that the safeguards available through registration procedures are
inadequate guarantors of quality control.

Practical issues

Regardless of political analysis, there are some common elements
evident in these developments. First, there is a marked shift from
individual working to teamworking. Secondly, there is an increasing emphasis on multidisciplinary working. Initially developed in community handicap teams, the concept has taken root
with widespread acknowledgement that the shared resources of
different disciplines are required to deliver the most effective
service to clients. Thirdly, the community, on which Seebohm
placed such emphasis, has been born again under the label
'locality' or 'neighbourhood'. The debate about patchwork in
social services has had some of the qualities of sterile theological
debate, but as in many theological debates the underlying truth is
what is important. Fourthly, the needs of carers are being afforded
increasing recognition both through shifts in formal service provision using day care and respite care more extensively, and
through links with informal care networks. Fifthly, the professional power vested in social workers is increasingly under
public scrutiny and challenge, with child abuse as the most obvious
area where public attention has been focused by a sustained
barrage of negative publicity.

The implications of these changes for social work's position within the personal social services are substantial. The most evident is a real question-mark over the future of social work. Within the large departments the privileged position which social workers have occupied as gatekeepers to departmental resources may not be tenable with the recognition of CSS as broadly equivalent to the CQSW, and the emergence of new patterns of service delivery. But if a plural system of welfare develops, with a flourishing private and voluntary sector, contracting out of services, competitive tendering and worker cooperatives, does come about, there will be a renewed interest in an external regulatory body to set standards for social work practice.

The skills required to produce teamwork which is flexible, locally based, responsive to consumer need and cost-effective are present within social work. The success of the Kent Community Care project is indicative of the potential if management structures can be established to support local flexibility. The reasons why management has found it difficult to offer that support are considered in the next chapter.

6

The Development of Managerialism

There are three targets for criticism in a bureaucratic structure when things go wrong – the individual worker, the organisation and the management. In social services, individuals have been called to account – sometimes in the fire of a public inquiry; organisations have changed, changed and changed again; and both the structures used to deliver services, and management have come under attack. The absence of consensus will be evident from the preceding chapters, and the attacks have come from diverse sources, sometimes mutually exclusive.

Managers have been criticised for being too removed from social work practice and too close to it, for being too concerned with value for money and too preoccupied with costs to see value, for being too directive and for failing to give a lead, for delegating too much and for failing to delegate at all. If social workers sometimes feel themselves the butt of unfair criticism, so too do those in managerial roles.

The Seebohm Report went into some detail about the qualities required of the Director of Social Services: 'an effective administrator, the leader of a group of people with widely differing backgrounds, able to take a broad and informed view of the needs the services ought to be meeting, and capable of looking outwards well beyond the limits of his own department and authority, and well into the future . . . will have to survey the needs of the area and plan the deployment of workers to meet them while at the same time taking care not to become remote from the problems of workers in the field and those whom the department is trying to help' (Seebohm 1968, para. 618).

Such a paragon would have faced a difficult task with a static workload. In reality there were four main areas of pressure fuelling expansion. First, the workload of staff increased dramatically reflecting a determined attempt to pursue an open-door policy and to improve access to social services. Secondly, the range of responsibilities was enlarged, with new legislative requirements relating to children in trouble, the chronically sick and disabled, playgroups and childminding and adoption. Thirdly, the social planning role sought by Seebohm led to closer working relationships with housing, education and health than had formerly prevailed. The voluntary sector too had to be involved in liaison arrangements. Fourthly, the size of agencies meant that advisory and coordinating roles developed to support and supplement line management arrangements.

While growth continued unabated, the qualities required of senior officers in social services were vision, an ability to plan, and good administrative skills. Setting up systems and establishing lines of communication were critical, as was supporting staff through the turbulent period of change. All these qualities are part and parcel of good management, but with the shift in the resource position the emphasis moved closer to the managerial skills more familiar in commerce and industry. Improved productivity, expressed as value for money, required economy, efficiency and effectiveness but the skills required to reorientate service provision were less evident.

How then did managers respond to the bombardment of referrals and the demand to ration resources more stringently? What techniques were available to them? Some of the responses were organisational, like intake teams specifically designated as a mechanism to handle high-volume/low-duration work, but many led to more sophisticated forms of rationing like priority ranking and workload management systems (Whitmore and Fuller 1980; Algie, Hey and Mallen 1981; Vickery 1977). The systems were often complex and time-consuming. Even where a model has been as well developed and validated as the Case Review method developed at the National Institute for Social Work, its impact on practice has been limited, with many social workers and managers resistant to the time-commitment involved in the process.

In the absence of a system, it has often been team managers at local level who have been forced to take responsibility for managing the flow of work. Allocation systems may be direct, with allocation of referrals from the team leader to individual workers. If this is adopted, the team-leader needs accurate and up-to-date knowledge of the current workload of individual team-members, of their special interests and aptitudes, and of any extraneous commitments – training courses, domestic crises – likely to affect the worker's ability to take on new referrals. Besides placing acute pressures on the team-leader, direct allocation has two disadvantages. First, it means individual workers have little sense of the pressures on the team as a whole. Secondly, it militates against a collective team-identity.

For these reasons, and social work's cultural disposition to discussion as a precursor to decision, group allocation meetings are widely used with the whole team involved in the process of allocation. As one respondent to the DHSS study commented, 'the allocation meeting allegedly allows a democratic choice. In reality it works out that the less strong-minded get lumbered' (Parsloe and Stevenson 1978, p. 73). Parsloe (1981) offers a number of helpful suggestions about allocation systems. Payne (1982) focuses more on the contribution that participation in the allocation process can make to team-building through a shared understanding of agreed priorities for work within the agency and the team, through developing formal and information specialisations and through mutual recognition of strengths and weaknesses.

A third system of allocation is based upon geographical patches. This is simple. It is clear, and it 'emphasises community responsiveness, but it may mean that specialised client needs are harder to meet, and variations in workload . . . can be hard to control.' (Payne, p. 57). The latter point is clearly shown in the report on Brent Social Services Department which noted enormous disparities in the volume of work carried even by adjacent patches following departmental reorganisation with one area receiving a child care referral for every 19 of its child population where in another it was one for every 160.

Essentially allocation is a tool to regulate the flow of work, and one which at times of explosive growth comes close to collapse. In the summer of 1987, the Cleveland inquiry into child sexual abuse showed a department unable to cope with a wholly unexpected surge in its workload. The pressures in Inner London mean that a number of authorities have been unable to allocate staff to work with children placed on the register of children at risk. These two examples show the problems faced by management in switching staff at short notice even to areas of the highest priority.

Child Care's Influence on Priorities

The impact of the Colwell case was discussed in Chapter 1. Not only did it put pressure on practitioners, it also highlighted the role of management – and that focus became sharper with subsequent child-abuse inquiries. The Colwell Report said, 'many of the mistakes made by individuals were either the result of, or were contributed to, by inefficient systems operating in several different fields, notably training, administration, planning, liaison and supervision. It is at the middle and higher levels that this case has shown to us that a great deal of thinking about child care is overdue' (Colwell 1974, p. 86). The responsibilities of the senior social workers were the focus of the Auckland Report in 1975 (Auckland 1975) which set out procedural requirements to be observed by senior social workers in child-abuse cases.

The emphasis has consistently been placed on administrative systems and procedures designed to safeguard the interests of children. The advent of Area Review Committees in 1974 and their successor Area Child Protection Committees, while producing guidance of variable quality, has provided a framework for inter-disciplinary discussion and agreement about procedures. The debate about the appropriate stance for social services authorities was taken into new territory by the findings of the Beckford inquiry and the Cleveland inquiry. Unhappily neither produced a consensus among practitioners, policy-makers and managers.

The sad case of Jasmine Beckford was given high profile coverage in the media. A black child had been placed with her parents after a period in foster case. Despite evidence of the father's potential for violence, the supervision afforded to Jasmine was inadequate to monitor the situation and certainly inadequate to safeguard the child from further abuse. The racial dimension and the implication that the desirability of placing black children with their black parents rather than mixed-race foster parents had influenced placement decisions, coupled with the stereotyping of Brent as a 'loony-Left' authority fuelled media interest in addition to the stark facts of the case. The Blom-Cooper report was widely publicised and its findings on management responsibility are clear. It found the social worker and her senior negligent for their 'failure to perceive the role of trustee-parent as paramount over the social work needs . . . of the Beckford parents' (Beckford 1985, p. 293). It highlighted procedural failures and questioned the adequacy of social work training in child care. The subsequent dismissal of the staff involved and their vilification in the popular press fostered the practice of defensive social work with increased use of Place of Safety Orders. The desire of social services managers to protect themselves has led to child-care policies giving priority to the elimination or, at least, minimisation of any risk. The logical consequence of these policies was evident in Cleveland.

The surge in child sexual-abuse referrals in Cleveland followed the appointment of two paediatricians applying a particular diagnostic technique. The social services authority acted on the diagnosis of the paediatricians and took Place of Safety Orders without any corroboration of the diagnosis until its residential resources were no longer able to cope and the public and political pressure became acute. The elimination of risk assumed precedence. Yet there are few certainties in dealing with human behaviour, and the task of social work is to mediate conflicting interests and reach a balanced view.

Fourteen years' experience of inquiries should have taught some lessons. But the lessons are not how best to safeguard the interests of vulnerable children. They are first, that social workers have consistently failed to communicate the delicacy and complexity of intervention in troubled families. Secondly, social workers remain a favourite target of the press, sometimes for being too interventive as in Cleveland, sometimes for following what Blom-Cooper termed the social worker's 'rule of optimism', hoping family circumstances would improve, and thus failing to intervene. Thirdly, if there is a tragedy, social workers can not always rely on their employing authority to represent their interests. Fourthly, senior management is now as vulnerable as practitioners. The Director in Brent was effectively forced to resign, and the Director in Cleveland has been heavily criticised.

The implications of those lessons for future policy are bleak. No legislative framework can safeguard children. Even if the balance were tilted towards child protection, there is abundant evidence that children in care remain vulnerable whether to abuse by staff in residential homes as in the Kincora scandal in Northern Ireland or to abuse by foster-parents. No procedural safeguards can offer a total guarantee of safety, although more could be done than is sometimes the case to minimise risk. Child-care tragedies will therefore continue to scar the psyche of the profession. But it is not enough to wring one's hands at the inevitability of problems, for there are managerial lessons which can be applied.

First, effective child-abuse work requires multi-disciplinary cooperation. Paediatricians, health visitors, social workers and GPs acting in concert can put together an effective package of inspection and monitoring. Secondly, management in all services has to be willing to work at that cooperation by ceding some of their cherished professional autonomy. Thirdly, the respective responsibilities of child-care workers need to be explicit and clearly understood and accepted by all parties to decision-taking. Fourthly, careful supervision can provide both a support to and a check on the staff with the responsibility to monitor and visit. Too often individual workers otherwise conscientious have failed to meet the basic requirement of seeing the child at risk. Fifthly, management policies should be known within the organisation, and communicated both orally and in writing. Reliance on folk wisdom or a presumption of a shared philosophy are wholly inadequate.

The value of procedural manuals is questionable. Many could cite examples of ring binders filled with instructions and guidance on most but never all eventualities which can confront social work staff. They consume an inordinate amount of staff time in their gestation and production, yet gather dust in the far recesses of area offices.

There is a need to have clear procedures but it is more productive to produce a few tightly drafted procedures on a few key areas – admission of children to care, children at risk, compulsory detention of mentally ill people, admission of elderly people to residential care – where the residence of the client may be changed, and find other means to promulgate good practice. through workshops, supervision and training programmes.

Alienation

So far this chapter has considered the problems in regulating work flow, and the pressures in management systems which have followed the child-abuse inquiries. Both were important influences in the emergence of a managerial culture in social services. But they brought a reaction in the emergence of a workforce finding it increasingly difficult to meet and identify with the aspirations of management.

Social work, by virtue of its commitment to addressing social problems, has a significant number of staff who believe that major economic and political changes are required to the existing social order if clients' needs are to be properly met. The rise in unemployment throughout the seventies, gathering pace in the eighties to an official peak of 3.2 million people, quickened the perception that the administration of palliatives through social casework had little to offer the poor. That view has a long history in social work, and management has tended to give it full rein, leaving it to individual workers how best to handle the dichotomy between concern for the individual in need and concern for the wider social issues raised by individual cases.

The commitment to social action felt by many social workers was reflected in trade union membership. The seventies saw a rapid growth in white-collar unionism as the lessons of the Heath Government's defeat by the miners were taken to heart by public sector unions. There were thus conflicting pressures on middle management with a critical, questioning workforce demanding participation in decision-making and with senior management pressing for financial restraint, manpower controls and clear statements of priorities.

Management flexed its muscles, and a rash of industrial disputes figured in the pages of social services journals. In Birmingham, a department was brought to a halt by a strike over a sacked social worker. The unhappy industrial relations climate reached its nadir with the social worker strikes in 1978 and 1979. These resulted from a protracted regrading claim which produced a series of local disputes with as many as fourteen local authorities on strike at the height of the dispute. The use of strike action was a serious blow to the professional pretensions of social work. By their actions social workers were identifying with industrial workers and using the same weapon of withdrawing their labour. Identification with the employee role was clearly dominant over the service ethic of professionalism. Nevertheless it was a minority of departments which figured in the action – and social work was deeply divided by the issue.

What the strike finally killed was the myth of the unified department sharing the same value system from fieldworker to Director. The imbalances of power and status and wealth within the departments were too great for shared values to surmount the sense of alienation felt by many staff at the remoteness of senior management. Just as the eighties had seen the power of industrial workers in sharp decline, with the miners serving as in the previous decade as the touchstone of government–labour relationships, so too one has seen a diminution in reported conflicts within social services. In part, this reflects the shift in power following successive pieces of trade union legislation, and in part the worsening unemployment situation and its impact on those with secure jobs.

The Mental Health Act 1983

Public sector trade unions have increased in sophistication. NALGO is represented on CCETSW. Its evidence to the Barclay Committee was extremely influential. Its tactics in relation to the Mental Health Act 1983 constitute an interesting case study of shifts in negotiating position, but a steadfastness in the face of pressure which produced radical change in relation to the assessment of approved social workers. The Act itself was the result of a very long gestation period. It constituted the first major reform of the law dealing with mentally ill people for a quarter of a century, and emphasised the rights of patients. One innovation explicitly designed to improve the standard of social work practice was the approved social worker, on whom would rest responsibility for compulsory admissions for assessment. The approved social worker was to be required to undertake specialist training, and to meet standards of competence in practice to be tested by examination.

The concept of the examination was fiercely resisted by NALGO on three main grounds. First, it argued that the existing qualification – the Certificate of Qualification in Social Work (CQSW) – was an adequate guarantor of professional standards, and that no further test of competence was appropriate. Secondly, it argued that the concept of approved social workers overvalued formal qualifications and discriminated against unqualified staff who had been carrying out mental welfare duties prior to the Act. Thirdly, it contended that an examination was a wholly inappropriate way to test competence in practice.

These three arguments were set against the combined forces of Parliament, which had used the Act to govern practice standards, the DHSS, CCETSW, the Association of Directors of Social Services and the British Association of Social Workers – all of which supported the idea of developing a post-qualification training and testing of approved social workers. On paper there should have been only one outcome to such an uneven struggle, but it turned out very differently.

NALGO, while occasionally caught by internal contradictions, tapped into a number of strands of disquiet. Once it had resolved an internal debate about whether to seek a higher level of remuneration for approved social workers, NALGO's stance appealed to the powerful egalitarian strand within social work, resistant to the concept of creating an elite within the workforce. It also won the support of those committed to generic practice and patchworking, for whom the advent of a specialist cadre posed organisational problems. And it touched a powerful undercurrent of anxiety about the validity of written examinations in social work. Of these, the last was the most significant. Despite trade union instructions, some social workers took the first examination and the high failure rate reinforced the fears expressed by NALGO. The failures included some of the most experienced mental health practitioners and the shock-waves were felt throughout the profession.

A tortuous series of negotiations took place to resolve the impasse. By blocking the examination, NALGO had effectively prevented local authorities from being in position to have a sufficient number of approved social workers in place for the implementation of that section of the Act. The DHSS was forced to allow a transitional period as the numbers taking successive examinations continued to fall. Under pressure, there were adjustments to the examination and, after a protracted struggle, the examination was dropped with the emphasis shifting to the content and quality of the specialised training rather than any formal testing of competence.

This episode illustrates a number of important truths about the widening gap between managers and the managed. Whatever the pretentions of professional bodies to speak for all social workers, in reality there is no sense of professional unity. Managers and workers are regarded as having very different interests. In the Mental Health Act issue, management sought to improve standards of practice and to secure an enhanced status for social work's contribution to mental health work. To social workers, however, the new provisions posed a threat to the status and value of the basic qualification, challenged established relativities within the work force, and introduced a test of competence of dubious validity. Some of the fears expressed by NALGO were undoubtedly misplaced, but they were nevertheless real in an employment climate devoid of trust.

While that issue has been resolved, it would be foolish to imagine that there are not and will not be other instances of managerial priorities proving at variance with those of the workforce. The impact of three terms of Conservative rule has switched the balance of power between the trade union movement and the Government. Public sector trade unions have lost membership, although the fall has been more acute in those unions with a high proportion of manual workers. The explosive growth in union membership of the seventies may be at an end, but the Mental Health Act dispute demonstrated the potential power of concerted action.

Economy, Efficiency and Effectiveness

The shift from a growth-orientation had begun before the Conservatives came to power in 1979. But for the first time management had to contemplate the prospect of real reductions in spending. At the same time as exerting pressure on the resources available for local government, central government asserted the importance of securing value for money. The creation of the Audit Commission, and the managerial credo of the three Es – economy, effectiveness and efficiency – further increased the emphasis on securing the maximum output from available resources.

Social services offered scope for some substitution of fieldwork and domiciliary services for residential services, for shifting young people from high-cost community homes to low-cost fostering, and for transferring financial responsibility for some in residential settings to social security. Many of these initiatives were in train prior to the advent of the Audit Commission, but undoubtedly the Commission has served to sharpen thinking about the use of resources.

The three Es are not, as is sometimes supposed, a seamless web of desiderata. Economy – providing a service at the least possible cost – is a requirement that is inherent in management. As a word, it does no more than imply the managerial imperative of eliminating waste in the provision of services. That imperative is no more and no less an imperative than was the case in the expansionist seventies. But economy pursued in isolation can be counter-productive to the pursuit of effectiveness – the relationship between outputs and inputs. Thus if there are six social workers in a child-care team with a total of twenty hours' clerical support, obliging the social workers to spend a substantial portion of their time in writing case records and routine clerical tasks, the total service will be more economical than if an extra clerical staff member were to be employed. But the employment of that worker would release expensive social worker time for the primary task of client contact, and thus be more effective. (This, of course, implies a value judgement about the efficacy of social worker contact which is discussed further below.)

Some of the methods used by management to achieve economy have been of a kind which have impaired rather than promoted effectiveness. A blanket or even a selective ban in filling vacancies is a regularly-used mechanism to slow down expenditure. It involves a wholly inefficient use of staff time in deploying arguments and energy to circumvent the ban. Manpower ceilings too can conflict with the strategic objectives of the organisation, and do not guarantee the most effective use of staffing resources. Imposing arbitrary percentage reductions – and calling them efficiency savings or cost improvements – is a tactic followed by the DHSS in the management of the National Health Service. While these are held to have had some success in eliminating waste, in reality the bulk of savings have been achieved through competitive tendering and energy conservation rather than through a wholesale reduction in expenditure levels. As the scope for these savings has been exhausted, the reductions are increasingly having an impact on core services.

Effectiveness is the extent to which an intervention achieves the desired outcome. It is separate from considerations of economy on the one hand and efficiency on the other. Thus if one is considering intensive community support of a vulnerable elderly person, the allocation of twelve hours' home-help time five days a week might well prove effective in keeping the elderly person at home. It would, however, neither be economic (as the cost would exceed that of a place in a residential setting), nor would it be efficient if the same desired objective could have been achieved with an input of five hours a day.

Despite this caveat, effectiveness is a critical issue for social work practice. A new scepticism is abroad, and social work can no longer rely on faith alone as the justification for its existence.

Social work practice has borrowed heavily from a number of disciplines. In the fifties and early sixties, the psychotherapeutic model was influential in shaping casework practice. This relied heavily on picking up verbal and non-verbal cues from the client, and using the worker–client relationship itself as the primary therapeutic instrument. As a consequence, the sensitivity and intuition of the worker were central to the success of intervention. Unhappily intuition and rigour do not sit easily together, and social workers' reliance on intuitive approaches has concealed the genuine knowledge base of the profession and militated against the development of a disciplined use of that knowledge base. Giller and Morris noted that social workers respond in an intuitive way to the difficulties presented by their clients, using theoretical justifications to buttress intuitive decision-making (Giller and Morris 1981). Parsloe and Stevenson found that 'social workers seemed to make (such) decisions without conscious thought and when pressed implied that they acted "by intuition" or that their behaviour was determined not by the individual client's need but by what they thought was the tradition of the local authority or by some practical feature' (Parsloe and Stevenson 1978, p. 339).

Research findings have consistently challenged the effectiveness of social work. Fischer (1976) suggested that social work was often ineffective, and on occasion produced deterioration in clients. Probation's IMPACT study found that reducing the caseloads of probation officers had no significant impact on the outcomes of clients on a number of indicators (Folkard 1975, 1976). Where social work intervention has achieved some modest success, it has

related to practical assistance, to work with the elderly with needs
not normally recognised as requiring social work help, and with
short-term focused intervention. There is, however, no research-
based case for social casework as therapy for the great majority of
the clientele of social services departments. Before one consigns
social work to the dustbin, one should note that Webb and Wistow
comment, 'none of the concern about the impact of social work
should be surprising. Very similar doubts have emerged about the
effectiveness of medicine and psychiatry' (Webb and Wistow
1987, p. 197).

One of the methodological problems in social work is the
measurement of outcome. In part, this can be blamed on the
fuzziness of objectives. Unlike management in an industrial concern which has ready yardsticks in productivity and profitability,
social work managers have no single touchstone of success by
which their efforts or those of their staff can be judged. The
volume of service, the inputs to the service, and even in some
services the outputs (meals on wheels, adaptations) can be measured, but the outcome eludes capture because it contains considerations of quality.

Performance indicators have been in use in the National Health
Service for several years and thus has developed a computerised
set of indicators which facilitates inter-authority comparisons.
But what are being compared? Expenditure, staff, turnover,
bed-stay, waiting lists can all be measured, analysed, cross-
analysed and tabulated. They tell the recipient nothing about
service quality. Whether the surgical interventions were necessary,
whether they cured the problem or whether they were so incompe-
tently performed that readmission was necessary, remain hidden
from view.

The DHSS has produced a list of similar indicators for personal
social services. Again, however, they focus on expenditure and
input measures, providing valuable comparative data on the
proportions of expenditure devoted to different client groups, the
mix between private and voluntary provision, the balance of
fieldwork, day care, domiciliary services and residential care, and
other indicators of trends in service mix, but they do not help
identify cost-effectiveness in service provision. Even the basic
question of whether one should have a high level of spending or a
low level of spending on a particular service is not susceptible of a

clear answer. In Northern Ireland, one Health and Social Services Board has double the level of home helps per thousand elderly of another neighbouring Board, yet its level of per capita expenditure on the elderly is lower than its neighbour because of a dearth of day care and residential provision. The home help service is less economical than that of the neighbouring authority but may be more effective.

The task facing management is to move beyond statistical indicators to the area of quality. Currently it is a reversion to the now unfashionable management-by-objectives approach which holds out some possibilities. One of the lessons which the task-analysis approach widely used in Certificate of Social Services schemes has taught social service managers is the importance of setting clear and defined objectives. Those objectives where possible should be measurable. Thus, 'to improve the quality of care in this home' is an aspiration-objective, but 'to ensure that each resident is toileted every two hours' or 'to ensure that each resident has a choice of activities each morning and afternoon' are defined and measurable objectives. While it takes time and thought to construct objectives in this way, it gives a purpose and rigour to social work intervention which is too often lacking.

The lessons of research can no longer be ignored. While intervention is unfocused it has no discernible impact upon clients. Where objectives are clear, and the intervention is time-limited, benefits can be achieved. Support and care are important social work values but they should be delivered where possible through community networks with social work intervention being primarily directed at change and development. There is a powerful counter-argument which asserts that social work's particular contribution is to offer care to groups in society which are disadvantaged, and that part of that care is not to make the demands that they change which are made by the rest of society. There is a danger that the managerial imperatives of effectiveness and efficiency will cause care to be devalued as an objective. The peculiar task of social services managers is to hold to core values while pursuing effective use of available resources.

The third of the three Es – efficiency – is the measure of the relationship between inputs and outputs. Thus it is possible to conceptualise a highly efficient service which uses a limited number of staff but by careful organisation of rotas, limits on the allocation of time to each client, and routine reporting and recording procedures, secures the maximum possible client-coverage for the lowest possible cost. The service, however, might be utterly ineffective in having no impact on the quality of life for the service recipient.

It is the contention of this chapter therefore that of the three Es, the key one of concern to social work is effectiveness. But effectiveness needs to be allied to efficiency if services are to be cost-effective, which is a legitimate managerial preoccupation. Before concluding this section, it is important to look at some of the recurring obstacles to cost-effectiveness. Some of the structural issues have already been examined in the context of the Audit Commission's report, but there are other constraints within the public sector which need to be identified. These are considered under the headings of budgets, incentives, risk-taking, and ethics.

Constraints on Effectiveness

Budgets

The cycle of annual budgets throughout the public sector militates against the development of effectiveness. First, it concentrates attention on inputs, the cash expended, rather than on the impact of a service. Secondly, the preoccupation with annual budgets sometimes makes it difficult to look at the medium-term effects of provision. Thirdly, there is a tendency to achieve results at least-cost to the budget without regard to effectiveness. The way in which resources have been switched from local authority budgets to social security budgets in relation to the funding of care in private and voluntary residential facilities is a clear example of the primacy of financial opportunities over planning.

Incentives

The present pattern of resource allocation does not build in incentives for the effective use of resources. Savings will often be clawed back centrally without benefiting the individual or facility responsible for making the savings. The absence of financial rewards or systematic performance appraisal means that initiative may go unrecognised. There are usually no penalties attached to overspending unless a consistent pattern is evident over several years.

Risk-taking

The culture of the public sector militates against risk-taking. A higher value is attached to consistency and soundness than to flair and innovation. The rewards from taking risks are slight compared with the costs of making mistakes. These organisational values are relevant and desirable if the environment is stable, but in a fast-changing world they constitute a restraint on development which militates against devising services which are flexible and responsive to consumer needs. The entrepreneurial skills sought have therefore to be grafted on to the public sector, involving methods borrowed from the private sector – performance review, monetary rewards geared to performance, brokerage of packages bought from a range of service providers – but the marriage remains an uneasy one, as two organisational cultures come into conflict.

Ethics

The cost-effective use of resources involves hard decisions. Specifically it involves decisions that individuals in need should not receive a service because the cost of providing the service is disproportionate to the benefit derived by the recipient. This raises important ethical considerations for social workers, who regard their role as promoting the welfare of individual clients. The tension between proportional justice, the need to secure consistency and equity in the distribution of service provision, and individual justice was noted by Parsloe and Stevenson: 'Social workers have a tendency to assume that the latter must always prevail and this notion may have gone unchallenged during training. In fact, the ethos of many courses probably gives it positive support' (Parsloe and Stevenson 1978, p. 357). The degree to which decisions of this kind are alien to the culture of social work and of the health care professions, and the pain caused to individual practitioners as a consequence, are often not fully appreciated by managers able to rationalise their decisions.

Managers have therefore found themselves in a world for which they were ill-prepared by their professional training, ill-equipped by experience after years of expansion, and ill-resourced in terms of access to appropriate management training. While a handful of post-qualifying courses in management have developed, there remains a double scepticism. First, can managers be trained for their task? Secondly, can social services management be split off from general management training or training for other local authority managers? The first question is easier to answer than the second.

Managers are made not born, despite the persistence of the contrary belief. Writing about management in 1981, I referred to the traits of the ideal leader and the seductive view that the social services would be improved if all managers had the drive and entrepreneurial flair of Freddie Laker and Lord Grade. Between writing and proofreading, Laker Airways collapsed and Lord Grade was dismissed! In the final text I substituted Sir Michael Edwardes and Lord Weinstock, but so transient is the currency of the trait theory that these names no longer command the same respect in business circles. The truth is simply that while training cannot make a bad manager into a good one, it can improve managerial performance at all levels and the manager who decries the value of training is both arrogant and foolish.

The nature of that training is less clear-cut. All management training tends to have a common core around the five management functions identified by Fayol in 1916 – planning, organising, coordinating, commanding and controlling. Some of the skills required are generic to the management function whether performed in an industrial, commercial or public sector context; and some are dependent upon the specific task. Thus knowledge of group processes, the limitations of budgeting, the impact of new technology, and the impact of managerial style are generic. The arcane mysteries of the rate support grant are highly relevant to local authority managers (although hardly to anybody else). The planning interrelationship with health, and the importance of coordinating field, day, domiciliary and residential services are specific to social services. Yet effective management training will need to address each of these issues.

The picture hitherto is somewhat bleak. A recent Local Government Training Board survey found that less than one in ten senior social services managers thought that their careers had a systematic pattern of development. Many authorities have developed their own management training on an in-house basis. The recent advent of video-assisted packages makes this a realistic undertaking for authorities, which can thus develop flexible and modular schemes for different staff groups.

The future pattern of management will clearly be determined by political decisions about organisation and structure. Some of the qualities which will be required of the new generation of welfare managers are already evident, and they differ markedly from those which have been paramount hitherto.

A useful summary of the changing world facing managers was supplied by Naisbitt in 1987. He identified the shifts as in Table 6.1.

Table 6.1 *Changes facing managers*

From	To
Industrial society	Information society
Forced technology	High-tech/high-touch*
National economy	World economy
Short term	Long term
Centralisation	Decentralisation
Institutional help	Self-help
Representative democracy	Participative democracy
Hierarchies	Networking
North	South**
Either/or	Multiple options

*High-touch is a reference to user-friendly information technology
**The North–South divide, while applied to the USA by Naisbitt, is equally applicable to both the UK and Europe.

It will swiftly be evident that this perceptive analysis has much to offer in the context facing social services, and that many of the points covered in the right-hand column have already been touched upon above.

Key factors will be the brokerage role, the ability to innovate, numeracy, and the capacity to cope with change.

Brokerage

The future will have only limited use for managers secure in hierarchical structures and in delivering institutional help. Increasingly the emphasis will be on skills which the Barclay Report described as social care planning. These involve putting together packages of care for vulnerable individuals or groups, which draw together resources from statutory services, voluntary organisations, informal networks of family, neighbours and volunteers. The ability to work with different agencies and to use diverse resources effectively will be a key element in the managerial task. This is not to discount the continuing need for counselling skills and work with vulnerable individuals, but to assert a shift in emphasis in service delivery and thus in the management task.

Innovation

If the organisational base is to change, the manager is going to be required to find new ways of responding to needs. Even if the organisational structure remained intact, the wider forces in society driving change have to be reflected in the pattern of provision. And new awareness of social problems as child sexual abuse follows child abuse and battered women into the forefront of public consciousness demands new responses.

Innovation does not just happen. It has to be stimulated and managed. It requires the commitment of time, and a flexibility which promotes horizontal communication. A vivid description of innovation in a social services team illustrates some of the processes and skills required (Currie and Parrott 1986).

Numeracy

Social work may be an art (or as Kenneth Brill, BASW's first General Secretary, termed it, a craft). It is certainly not a science. Yet there are valid reasons for suggesting that numeracy will become an important factor in management. First, the cash nexus whether constructed in terms of annual budgets, or the three Es, means that management has to be aware of and able to use finance. Secondly, the emphasis placed above on effectiveness can best be demonstrated by using numbers as proxies for performance. These can be used in developing ranking scales like those established to measure behavioural skills of people with disabilities as a means of measuring change. Thirdly, the use of information technology will make the manipulation of statistical data an essential element of managerial performance.

Coping with change

The focus hitherto has been on stimulating change, but it is important to recognise that change creates its own stresses both for individuals and for the organisation. Bennis and Nannis (1985) suggest four roles for leaders in the change process – the generation of a shared vision of the desired future, an understanding of the culture of the organisation and an ability to reshape it, the positioning of the organisation in the environment and the establishment of links between the organisation and the environment, and the readiness to make changes to help organisations to handle newly-emerging issues.

Of these the first two are of critical importance, for confronted with change, organisations tend to retreat into defensive paralysis because of the insecurity of the environment. Tackling that by creating confidence in a shared vision is important. With the scale of change facing social services, it is necessary to build on the strengths of caring and flexibility within the organisation and apply those to changed structures. Maintaining a care for staff has not always been given the priority it deserves in the large departments. If the monoliths are to be more fragmented, one plus-point may be the greater intimacy and personal contact of smaller flexible structures.

What does all this mean for future management structures? The argument set out above is that social work management is unlikely to find the next twenty years as stable as the preceding two decades. Despite the numerous challenges and threats experienced in that period, they have been handled in the context of a relatively stable organisation. That stability is now under threat, and the trends in society identified by Naisbitt suggest that managers will have to learn new skills to cope with the rapidity of change in their environment. One way of conceptualising that task is to think of management in terms of the loose-fit/tight-fit metaphor.

The delegation of resource allocation and operational decision-making will become loose. Looser too will be the control over the mix of public and private, formal and informal support systems. Tighter, however, will be the overall control of finance, the determination to seek quality – perhaps in the form of prescribed standards, and the control of the operating procedures and systems in the organisation which shape the culture.

7

Health and Social Services: Partners or Rivals?

There is a long history of tension between the health care professions and those services for which local authorities have had responsibility since 1948. As so often it is instructive to look at the Seebohm Report to trace the basis for the divergent views of the two occupational groups.

The pattern of provision showed overlapping and sometimes interchangeable responsibilities. As early as 1918 the Maternity and Child Welfare Act had identified the contribution which local government services could make to preventive health by empowering the provision of a home help service following the birth of a child. Until 1946 the responsibility for the care of the mentally disordered was divided between local authorities and voluntary hospitals. After 1948 Health departments within the local government structure employed social workers and other staff to meet the mental health needs of the community.

The Seebohm Report was highly critical of the lack of coordination between different services. Its central recommendation of a social services department was, however, extremely unpopular with medical interests. As the Report itself recognised, it had the effect of removing half their staff and a substantial part of their budget, contacts and interests in the local authority service. The status of the Medical Officer of Health was called into question and his authority on welfare issues subordinated to that of the Director of Social Services, who had no medical qualification.

The early years of social services were characterised by a number of skirmishes between the infant departments and medical colleagues. Unfavourable comparisons were drawn between the burgeoning bureaucracies of social services and the personal service offered under the aegis of the former health departments. Gradually relationships were forged with new staff and the two services started to look at ways in which they could best cooperate.

The ten-year plans required from local authorities by Sir Keith Joseph in 1973 were the first test of working relationships at a policy level, since they were intended to interlock with the health service planning cycle being established with the 1974 reorganisation of the NHS. Reorganisation is never helpful to the achievement of successful working relationships. New contacts have to be made, new relationships established and new roles worked out at the same time as ensuring that services are maintained. But as those links were forged it became increasingly evident that goodwill alone would not produce collaboration. Before considering the impact of the joint planning and joint finance machinery that was established it is worth examining the structural impediments that remained to blight collaborative working.

These can be summarised under four heads: policy differences, planning and budget differences, professional differences and cultural differences.

Policy differences

Put at its crudest, the interests of the health service and local authority services are very different. Expressed in the abstract in terms of the health and welfare of the community no divergence exist, but when it comes to the harsh realities of spending priorities and competition for limited resources, a different and more accurate picture emerges. When an elderly person who has been supported in the community by a network of provision has to be admitted to hospital care, there is likely to be a net increase in public resources devoted to the care of that person, but there will also be a substantial reduction in the spending by social services. Conversely when a long-stay mentally handicapped person is discharged from hospital care to the community it is the local authority which has to increase its expenditure and the savings occur in hospital budgets. What exists in reality is an interlocking pattern of services with transfers of responsibility often unaccompanied by a concomitant transfer of funding.

There is a tension within the health care sector. This is the tension between the demands of the acute sector of care based in District General Hospitals and long-stay services for mentally ill, mentally handicapped, and elderly people. Looking at the balance between spending on these different sectors of health care, it is clear which has wielded the greater influence. While there are undeniably pressures on acute care, compounded by the need to improve throughput and to reduce the length of bed-stay, the standard of care and the level of equipment available are indicative of the priority given to acute care. Contrast those services with the staff ratios evident in long-stay hospitals and consider the sorry sequence of enquiries into neglect and abuse of patients in such settings. The consistent failure of the health service adequately to resource the less fashionable and less prestigious areas of care is all too evident.

It is precisely that imbalance in resource distribution which makes it difficult to secure the resource transfer to accompany patients discharged to the community. The patients discharged are often the least dependent, who make the least demands on hospital staff. Yet left behind are the more difficult and more demanding patients. The temptation to use discharges as a means of improving staffing ratios by holding on to staff and money is therefore extremely powerful. Thus even when there is agreement on the strategic direction of change, there are real problems in securing the implementation in a way which satisfies all interests.

Planning and budgeting differences

The planning cycles of the two services are very different. After the initial attempt to align them at the time of the ill-fated ten-year plans, there has been a marked divergence between the two. While the Health Service has stuck doggedly to a strategic planning cycle of five- and ten-year plans, the time horizons of local authorities and their ability to engage in forward planning have progressively shrunk. The ten-year plans were succeeded by the requirement to submit a planning statement. This was a three-year forward look at local authority social services. The system lasted only two years, as the financial position of local government, reflecting the overall economic position, became steadily bleaker. 'There was, however, a curious element of the self-fulfilling prophecy about the planning process. The analysis of

LAPS returns was fed back to local authorities. The average of the returns was then used in DHSS Planning Guidelines which in turn were used by many authorities as the basis for their LAPS returns since returns were required at a time when budget plans had not been formulated' (Bamford 1982, p. 121). And with the advent of the Conservative Government with its less sympathetic attitude to public welfare provision the planning statements were abandoned altogether.

The lack of congruence between the planning requirements imposed by the one government Department is eloquent testimony to the degree of truly joint planning at central government level. It was further compounded by the lack of fit between the budget cycles of the two authorities. Thus while local authorities lived on an annual cycle, and service developments had to be approved as part of the budget-making process, the health service, despite its apparently cumbrous planning cycle, was often able to act more swiftly by juggling recurring and non-recurring monies and by the lack of any obligation to identify service developments several months in advance of implementation.

There is a reason for the mismatch described above. It relates to the capital programme of the Health Service and the scale of capital and revenue finance required to sustain major projects like hospitals where the capital cost can run into scores of millions and the revenue up to ten million for a modest District General Hospital. Financial allocations of that dimension have to be planned over a much longer time-scale than local authority capital schemes. By contrast, smaller schemes – and these were usually the stuff of joint finance discussions between the two services – could be dealt with more speedily by decision-making processes in the health service.

Professional differences

The professional differences can be seen most clearly in the position of consultants within the Health Service. They stand unchallenged at the pinnacle of the structure, but their position derives from sapiential authority – the authority that comes from the possession of exclusive knowledge – rather than a formal location at the top of a decision-making hierarchy. Indeed the irony is the relative lack of direct involvement of clinicians in management decisions whilst they exercise immense influence in other ways. The advent of General Managers following the first Griffiths Report (1983) can be regarded as an attempt to break through the stranglehold exercised by medical interests on decisions within the acute sector of medicine. The local government model of political accountability militates against the development of professional power in this way, and social work lacks the system of self-regulation which is the basis of the medical and nursing professions' claims within the health care structure.

The influence of medical vested interests is strongest in the acute sector of medicine. The emphasis is upon curative medicine, the treatment and restoration to full health of the sick. The contribution which community services both within health care and within the local authority can make to prevention of ill-health has been under-appreciated and under-resourced until recently, when a more assertive Health Education movement has been evident.

As a consequence, with the exception of the minority of clinicians working at the interface with community services (like geriatricians and paediatricians), the majority of consultants found it hard to see why health service resources should be earmarked for use by social services in the way that joint finance was set up. This was compounded by the pressure on resources which has characterised the last ten years, leading to ward closures and growing public awareness of the problems facing the health service.

Cultural differences

The impact of local democratic control was a severe culture shock for many health service managers. Not only did it introduce a new and unpredictable element into decision-taking but it constituted an exposure to the rude world of politicised argument which was foreign to them despite the presence of some elected members on health authorities. The impact of ratecapping, and even in those authorities which avoided it, the acute awareness of the marginal costs of extra rate-borne expenditure, led to an increase in the share of joint finance going to health authorities. The vagaries of local government finance militated against the rational approach to joint planning which collaborative arrangements were supposed to produce.

Virtually all authorities that provide social services lose grant if they increase spending in real terms . . . those authorities that wish to develop their community care policies must either make equivalent cuts elsewhere in their budgets, or they must transfer a disproportionately high burden of costs onto local ratepayers. . . . Hence, the system used to control expenditure can penalise local ratepayers in authorities implementing Government policy and saving money for the NHS into the bargain (Audit Commission 1986, p. 34).

In a rigorous critique of the medical model of health, Bywaters argues that these structural difficulties are only part of the reason for continuing tension between social work and medicine. Suggesting that health policy should be concentrated more on prevention through attention to social and environmental factors, he notes that 'social work finds itself at odds with medicine in its central belief in a respect for the client's self-knowledge and right to choice, and in its growing recognition of the value of mutual support and exchange. Medical expectations of patient passivity fit uneasily with social work objectives of a self-directed and empowered clientele' (Bywaters 1986, p. 670).

This tension finds expression in very different attitudes to client-access to records. A far more restrictive approach is evident from health care interests, both medical and paramedical, than is evident in social services.

Collaborative Structures

The 1973 NHS Reorganisation Act placed a statutory obligation on both health and local authorities to cooperate. Joint Consultative Committees were set up in 1974 to advise 'on their performance in cooperative activities and on the planning and operation of services of common concern' (DHSS, 1977). This member-level structure was mirrored by an officer-level structure of Joint Care Planning Teams. The Royal Commission on the National Health Service, reporting in 1979, noted a number of criticisms of these arrangements. 'The main complaint has been that responsibility for the individual patient or client is unclear, and that as a result he or she may fall between two parts of what should be an integrated service' (DHSS 1979).

The Commission identified three proposals for change. These were the transfer of the Health Service to local government, the transfer of personal social services to the health service and the transfer of responsibility for particular client groups to one service or the other. While the first of these may seem a remote possibility, the Commission pointed out that until 1948 most hospitals were provided by local authorities. The Commission's rejection of the proposal, despite conceding advantages in terms of democratic accountability, was based on the strength of feeling against the proposal from the professions, fearing interference with clinical freedom, and the financial implications of changes of that magnitude. Interestingly the door was left open for eventual joint administration of the two services if a regional tier of Government were to develop in the future.

The option of transferring social services to the health service was supported by the British Medical Association and the Royal College of Nursing. Noting that any such move would be strongly resisted by local authority interests, the Commission acknowledged that by itself such a shift would not achieve integrated planning of the two services. Education and housing would remain with the local authority, and linkages there might be impaired by any change to social services. Most important, it was accepted that the majority of clients of social workers came from sources other than health-related referrals and these functions could be disrupted by transfer to the health service.

The proposal to transfer lead responsibility to one service or the other has a familiar ring about it and was to resurface in the Audit Commission's report seven years later. While this would have the advantage of clearly identifying responsibility for particular groups, it would divide the professions, with nurses and doctors working in local government and social workers in the health service. Endorsing local experiments with this option was as far as the Commission was willing to go in the face of likely professional resistance.

One experiment in which the Royal Commission expressed considerable interest was that of the model adopted in Northern Ireland where health and social services had been integrated since 1973. In the Province the advent of direct rule had made a radical recasting of local government responsibilities inevitable, but the particular form of change adopted and its success or failure has important lessons for the rest of the United Kingdom.

The Northern Ireland Model

Northern Ireland has four Health and Social Services Boards. The majority of Board members are nominees of the Secretary of State for Northern Ireland. They represent a balanced grouping of professional interests, trade union interests and employer interests. In addition there are a number of members nominated by the District Councils in the area. It should be noted that although the councils are the forum for a deal of political pointscoring, their effective powers are minimal, being restricted to leisure and refuse-collection.

At officer-level there is an Area Executive Team consisting of Chief Officers including the Director of Social Services.* The team is headed by a General Manager but, unlike England, Wales and Scotland, there is no system of Unit General Managers. At Unit-level the management responsibility is carried by a multi-disciplinary group of second-line officers. Both at the Area Executive Team and at Unit-level there is medical representation of GPs and consultants but the medical representatives have no management authority over their colleagues nor can they commit their colleagues to a particular course of action. This can be extremely convenient when unpopular decisions have to be taken!

The system in Northern Ireland has two major structural advantages over that prevailing in England and Wales. Not only is social service provision clearly built into the joint structure, but there is also no separation of the family practitioner services. The opportunities for the development of effective primary care are therefore much enhanced. Whether full benefit has been taken of these advantages is more doubtful.

The introduction of the integrated service was not universally welcomed. Social services interests were apprehensive about their ability to compete on equal terms with health care colleagues in the allocation of resources. At a time when other parts of the United Kingdom were engaging in a rapid expansion of services it was feared that the historic under-resourcing of personal social services would continue. To meet these anxieties the Department of Health and Social Services agreed to an earmarked allocation of finance for social services. Unlike England and Wales, where the allocation of resources is a matter for local determination, North-

*In 1989 the Government published its White Paper, *Working for Patients*, which envisaged major changes.

ern Ireland is closer to that of a Regional Health Authority with a fixed sum of public finance available for distribution between the four Boards with the Department playing the role of the regional authority.

The size of the Province, with a total population just over one-and-a-half million, is a relevant factor in any analysis of the working of the health care system in Northern Ireland. It means that there is a much closer relationship between the civil servants at the Department and senior managers in the Boards than would be true of the relationship between Regional Health Authorities and the Department in England. There is also closer Ministerial involvement in the minutiae of service delivery with the Minister personally chairing the accountability reviews held each year between the Department and Boards.

The decision to give an earmarked budget to social services did indeed guarantee a very rapid build-up of social services provision from its low initial starting-point. The expansion took place at a time of rapid growth of public expenditure. The political situation in Northern Ireland meant that expansionist policies were pursued for several years after Anthony Crosland signalled the end of the party for local government elsewhere. It has also influenced attitudes to employment. While shedding labour is a predictable response to financial pressure on the public sector, the appalling unemployment situation in the Province and the fears of the consequences on the streets of increasing yet further the numbers out of work has meant that strategies like competitive tendering to reduce costs have been much delayed in reaching Northern Ireland.

By 1978 it was felt that social services' position was sufficiently well established to allow the earmarked budget to be replaced by a single allocation to Boards, allowing them to choose their own priorities. Like all allocation processes involving central and local government the true picture is not quite as clear as the statement above might imply. Central Government finds it very difficult to cede control over priorities to local decision-taking in England and Wales. It is more difficult to do so in a small community when the architects of policy are not insulated from pressure from Board members, local politicians and the media. In practice therefore the role of the Department is one in which it acts as custodian of central Government interests either by formally indicating particular areas where Boards are expected to initiate new developments or by top-slicing some of the overall allocation in order to fund specific developments separately.

The difficulties in relationships which were identified above as one of the contributory factors to problems in bringing about effective collaboration were ascribed in part to cultural differences between health care professionals and those from a social services background. The years in which social services had a separate budget served to compound and exaggerate those differences. Three areas of difference can readily be identified.

First, the emphasis placed by social work staff on client participation, whether in terms of recording or reviews or planning, sat uneasily with a traditional reliance upon professional decision-making with decisions taken on behalf of clients. Secondly, the majority of day care and residential facilities operated by social services have minimal input from other health care professions and operate on a uni-disciplinary basis. That adds to the sense of being separate from the rest of the organisation.

Thirdly, the attitudes shown by social services sometimes cause bewilderment in other parts of the organisation. The logo of the Board on transport is a badge of pride to the ambulance service yet a continuing source of anxiety to social services staff who see it as potentially stigmatising to clients, particularly so if it refers to hospital transport. Bulk-buying of foodstuffs may make good economic sense in the context of a hospital. In a children's home it is anathema. And risk-taking is another area of conflict, especially in relation to former long-stay patients. In pursuit of a philosophy of normalisation, social workers are ready to let clients attempt activities on their own as part of the necessary process of development. The culture of the institution is still evident in many colleagues who would favour a more protective and paternalistic attitude.

The main benefits obvious to those who have struggled through the web of collaborative structures on the mainland are the unified mechanism for joint planning, the integrated system of finance and the links at primary care level possible within an integrated model. But even here the potential is a long way from realisation. The planning systems in the four Boards do draw together representation from a range of professional groups. There is an acute consciousness of the importance of developing multi-disciplinary planning. But much of the planning stops short at the level of representation. There is not a readiness to view the total resources available to the Boards as an integrated and interlocking provision. Thus while a joint group will plan services to the elderly and map out the needs for domiciliary care, no attempt is made to aggregate the very substantial resources deployed by those services offered by social services like the home help service and meals on wheels with the services of district nursing and health visiting. At an individual case level, particularly in the sensitive area of child-abuse, efforts will be made but there is no systematic look at the balance of care to ascertain where additional resources could most effectively be used for the benefit of the elderly population. A crude bidding system operates in which different disciplines vie with each other for incremental growth and from which shared working is almost wholly absent.

The financial structure does undoubtedly make it very much easier to effect resource transfers since they are transfers only from one part of the Board to another. But resource transfers require the agreement of the sector of the Board giving up resources as well as the concurrence of the sector acquiring new responsibilities. It is here that the simplicity of the structure runs foul of professional vested interests. No part of the Health Service is so generously funded that it can readily agree to give up money to another area. Thus the rough and ready dowry system in operation in England in relation to mental handicap and mental health services assumes that patients carry with them resources equivalent to the average unit cost of a hospital in-patient. In Northern Ireland the honourable attempt to transfer the appropriate sum with the closure of wards and units, rather than with individual patients, provides limitless scope to juggle staff and resources to minimise the actual cash transfer.

With admirable regard to the lessons available from community care projects in Britain, the Department established bridging funds to enable Boards to develop services in the community in advance of the release of funds from hospital closures. Within a few months of these bridging funds being made available the acute financial pressures on services led the Department to suggest raiding those funds to relieve pressures caused by the underfunding of pay awards. That mixed message has been well understood as a statement that bridging finance is a good idea if – and only if – it can be afforded.

The net effect is therefore that despite the right structures to facilitate a coordinated approach to community care the very fact of integration makes it far more difficult to achieve a 'ring-fence' to protect the financial resources needed to make community care a reality rather than a slogan.

Sadly the third advantage of integration – the links at primary care level – reveal a similarly bleak picture. Of course there are numerous examples of effective collaboration between workers at primary care level, but what is so dismaying is that the organisation of services does nothing to facilitate that cooperation. There is no coterminosity between neighbourhood nursing patches and social services areas. There is little shared working with social workers alongside community nurses, and a consequent blurring of boundaries between the two. Instead one finds a rigid demarcation line between the professions with fierce competition for the middle ground in terms of community provision for mentally handicapped and mentally ill people.

This dismal picture may sound too gloomy for those struggling with the problems of yelling across the divide between health and social services. The level of patients in long-stay care in Northern Ireland and the slow rate of discharges despite the structural advantages tell their own story.

There are, however, lessons which can be learned from the experience in Northern Ireland. The first and the most important is that by changing structures one does not change attitudes. The professional culture is particularly resistant to the impact of structural change. Prescribing the imposition of general management at unit-level as the remedy for the problems would therefore be unproductive and would further muddy the waters in terms of lines of accountability. The reforms proposed by Griffiths have to be seen in this context. He recognised that a revised structure will not in itself achieve change unless it is buttressed by shared organisational and professional commitment.

How then can this commitment be obtained? Some clues were offered by the Audit Commission in its analysis of successful community care initiatives discussed in Chapter 4. That has been supplemented by work initiated by the King's Fund and contained in its submission to the Griffiths inquiry (Kings Fund 1987).

There were four key components identified in the King's Fund paper which overlap to some extent with those noted by the Audit Commission. They were:

1 *Clear values and principles* The importance of a clear and coherent view of the future shape of services is evident, and achieving that clear view may require the strong local champions of change mentioned by the Audit Commission.

2 *Consideration of the views of service recipients* To some extent this mirrors the neighbourhood focus indicated by the Audit Commission but it has also to be noted that the professional orientation of existing services is not responsive to consumer interests. A culture change has therefore to be brought about in which consumers are given a direct involvement in service planning rather than a token opportunity to comment on plans drawn up by professionals.

3 *The involvement of professional knowledge and skill* Discussing this comment Murphy notes, 'a conservative profession does not like to see change for change's sake, but it is worth planning at a slower pace to ensure medical commitment' (Murphy 1988).

4 *Access to all the usual community services* Here the King's Fund identified the need to ensure genuine integration by securing full participation of persons discharged to the community in the regular services available to all members of the community. The normalisation philosophy of care developed in relation to mental handicap services has been influential in shaping attitudes to provision.

Just as the recommendations of the Firth Report were put on ice pending the receipt of the Griffiths Report so too have decisions on Griffiths had to await the findings of the major internal review of health service funding taking place at senior ministerial level. The views put forward by Griffiths, however, have to be tested against the difficulties already identified in securing effective collaboration. Would they work? Would they improve the quality of service received by patients and clients?

The Griffiths Report

The analysis and conclusions reached by Griffiths repay careful study, for they indicate aspects of the likely future even if parts of the report may prove too much to swallow in the face of political and professional objections.

The key recommendations may be divided into issues of responsibility, of finance, of coordination and of training.

Responsibility

Local government received unexpected endorsement from the report with its unequivocal view that social services should be responsible for identifying people with community care needs in their area, and for the development and management of packages of care to meet the needs of the individuals. That approach was entirely consistent with the thrust of the Audit Commission report. What was more surprising was the redefinition of the health service role coming from the Deputy Chairman of the NHS Management Board, Sir Roy Griffiths. This should

> continue to be the provision of health care. In broad terms this involves investigation, diagnosis, treatment and rehabilitation undertaken by a doctor or by other professional staff to whom a doctor (sometimes a general practitioner) has referred the patient. In addition, health authorities have important responsibilities for health promotion and the prevention of ill-health. Health authorities should not provide services which fall outside this definition (Griffiths 1988, p. 15).

This effectively would redraw the existing boundary between the health service and local authority by reversing the 1974 reorganisation, at least in relation to parts of the community nursing services. The proposal that the social services authority would be responsible for the assessment of applicants for residential *and* nursing home care makes excellent sense in view of the accumulating evidence that there is a marked degree of overlap between residents in nursing settings and those in residential care homes, but it will assuredly draw criticism from the nursing profession.

While there may be some minor deviations from the primacy accorded to local government by Griffiths, it is hard to see any alternative pattern. Griffiths was politely dismissive of the lead authority concept or the allocation of responsibility based on the client group concerned promoted as options by the Audit Commission as creating 'disruption and turbulence . . . to no real benefit', and asserted, 'I firmly believe that the major responsibility for community care rests best where it now lies: with local government' (Griffiths 1988, p. 11).

Care is complex because the needs of individuals are infinitely variable. No profession or setting has a monopoly of wisdom and there will continue to be a need for close cooperation in delivering high-quality care in the community. What the Griffiths Report has provided is a framework 'in which local responsibility for delivery of community care is clear beyond doubt' (p. 10).

Financial mechanisms

While the affirmation of confidence in local authorities has been greeted like manna from heaven, the same cannot be said of the financial aspects of the Report. There is no view within the Report about the appropriate level of funding for community care. The purpose of the Report was to examine how resources were used rather than whether they were adequate but Griffiths' silence has attracted some criticism.

Greater concern has resulted from the suggested recasting of public funding. The Report suggests three sources of funding for social services – joint finance which should be made over wholly to social services, the Community Care grants section of the Social Fund, and social security support for those in residential care – in addition to that financed through local government. While joint finance may be nearing the end of its useful life as a pump-priming device, the other two changes are more controversial and evoke suspicions of Greeks bearing gifts.

The Social Fund is the most regressive act of social security policy for fifty years. Community Care grants are the sweetener designed to persuade doubters that the reforms would improve rather than impair the prospects of resettlement in the community for long-stay patients and other vulnerable groups. Yet the application of a cash limit, the absence of appeal procedures, and the lack of any entitlement to assistance, render the grants only marginally less objectionable than loans under the Social Fund. Social services agencies played a leading role in the sustained campaign against the Fund. It would be impossible for them now to embrace with enthusiasm the suggested transfer of resources and responsibility.

There are two basic objections. First, community care grants cover a spectrum of needs, including those of client groups excluded from consideration by Griffiths. The level of funding is inadequate to meet all the needs identified. Local authorities will therefore be reluctant to incur the odium of operating a grossly flawed system not of their making. The second and even more fundamental objection is that responsibility for that part of social security provision would wholly blur the dividing line between income-maintenance and social work.

There is nothing preordained about the existing division. It is the result of the separation of welfare and income maintenance functions in the 1948 legislation. Many Western European countries have substantial numbers of social workers employed in their social security offices combining in one person the assessment of financial and welfare needs. In the USA, caseworkers are to be found at the heart of the welfare system providing payments in cash or kind. In the United Kingdom, however, the separation is jealously guarded and social workers would be united in resisting moves to engage them in responsibility for the administration of cash payments. There are three reasons for the strength of feeling generated by the issue.

First the separation has enabled social workers to act as advocates for their clients without having to be concerned about the financial consequences of successful advocacy. Secondly, the task of building relationships is difficult enough without the balance of the relationship being distorted by the cash-giving power of the worker. The concept of empowerment and partnership which is at the core of the new professionalism would be undermined by the workers having such absolute power over the client. Thirdly, some workers would regard money issues as a distraction from their primary task of strengthening the coping capacities of the client.

If Community Care grants are unlikely to be greeted with enthusiasm, the same has to be true of the Griffiths proposals in relation to social security funding. Here a deceptively simple proposal designed to build-in incentives for the development of community care is envisaged. Instead of the present two-tier level of social security benefit dependent on whether the recipient is in residential care or a nursing home, Griffiths proposes a residential allowance financed through social security but 'limited to a fixed maximum sum, substantially lower than at present, payable on the present basis with the rest being paid by the social services authority against an assessment of need for care' (p. vii).

The intention of the proposal is to put the social services authority in a position of financial neutrality so that decisions about care are not distorted by financial considerations for the authority, and so that individuals are not placed in a form of accommodation providing a higher level of care than is required. The proposal would exclude the perverse incentives within the present system which operate to reduce health and social services spending when people move into residential care, while often increasing public expenditure in total. It could, however, build-in a negative consequence by virtue of the financial imposition on social services of the extra costs of residential care. This could lead some local authorities to substitute lower-cost but arguably less appropriate day and domiciliary services for some clients. There is no doubt that the requirement of meeting the topping-up cost of residential care will cause social services to look critically at their use of this resource.

The most radical departure from current financial structures comes in one of the central recommendations of the Report where a new system of percentage grant is proposed. This would be a specific grant to social services authorities based on available indicators of need. Local government has a longstanding aversion to specific grants, believing that individual local authorities are best placed to judge their own priorities, and could be relied upon to resist any extension of specific grant, even if no explicit central control of spending priorities was indicated. Griffiths indicated, however, that plans will have to be approved by the DHSS. Acknowledging fears that this would be seen as an extension of central control, Griffiths wrote, 'the control is actually intended to be a minimum consistent with there being any national policy in this area and is designed simply to ensure and evidence at local level that the matter is being taken seriously and that the frame-work of collaborative care is established and working' (p. viii).

Coordination

The need for coordination is identified at three levels of policy and decision-making – ministerial, strategic and individual. At each level the report contains proposals to secure greater clarity and coordination of effort.

While some critics have seen the suggestion of a Minister for Community Care as a blatant populist bid for headlines, the Report is unusually explicit about the tasks to be undertaken by the Minister. It is to 'promulgate a definition of community care values and objectives to guide its development' and to 'be responsible for ensuring that national policy objectives were consistent with the resources available to public authorities charged with meeting them and for monitoring progress towards their achievement' (p.16). A central implementation team is proposed to support the Minister.

To provide the strategy at local level the development of plans is a task for local social services authorities in consultation with health, housing and voluntary bodies. There is an important caveat which may make the recommendations controversial with both professional and trade union interests. The role for social services authorities is to shift from an emphasis on direct service provision to a role of designing, organising and purchasing services, making the maximum feasible use of the voluntary and private sectors.

This shift of emphasis has profound implications for the shape of services in the future. Social services authorities 'should seek to negotiate the best possible prices for individual places in residential and nursing home care, reflecting the particular care needs of the individuals concerned and local market conditions. They should look rigorously at the comparative costs of domiciliary services ... and seek out the most efficient services there too, whether from the private voluntary or statutory sectors' (p. 21).

There is a culture shift required from local authorities, to embrace with enthusiasm the task of weighing their own services against those provided by the private sector. As the discussion of Westland's critique of the Audit Commission in Chapter 4 indicated, there are numerous practical problems posed by the introduction of competing providers in an imperfect market.

At the point of service, delivery changes are proposed which appear more likely to secure widespread acceptance. These are, first, the identification for each person with community care needs of a named individual as the primary contact with public services, who would have the responsibility of advising the social services authority of any changes in the individual's circumstances. Improving the access of service-users is given high priority in the report, with the need for readily available information about services and how to get them.

Secondly, in cases where a significant input of public resources is necessary, a 'care manager' is proposed to oversee the process of assessment and reassessment and manage the resulting action. The influence of the Kent Community Care scheme can be seen in this proposal which would require the care manager to have accurate knowledge of the costs of providing various packages of care.

Training

This has been considered in Chapter 4 but it is important to note that the consequences of the Report for the current organisation and training of all the professions engaged in community care could be immense. The tenor of the Report is unsympathetic to the traditional aspirations of the professions to improve the standards of training and practice, and to establish a recognised role requiring qualifications from the postholders. As well as criticising the insularity of training for the various professional groups, Griffiths comments, 'there may in fact be a tendency to over elaborate, both as to the professional input and the training required. Many of the needs of elderly and disabled people are for help of a practical nature (getting dressed, shopping, cleaning). There is need for a new multi-purpose auxiliary force to be given limited training and to give help of a practical nature in the field of community care' (p. ix).

This proposal is strikingly similar to the Audit Commission idea of 'community carers' to undertake frontline support of dependent people. The reference to the recruitment of school-leavers, and experiments with YTS trainees does not suggest that moves to professionalise caring would find ready support from Griffiths.

Conclusions

It would be foolhardy to make firm predictions of the future when it is clear that the Government itself is undecided on the future direction and shape of public health and welfare provision. Yet equally it would be foolish to ignore the indications of the preferred future in Government thinking, even if it will take several years to reach that future.

The third Tory victory has put on the political agenda the possibility of change in services which had seemed so deeply rooted in the postwar consensus that their values and structures had not been challenged. The primacy of the market or at least the creation of a proxy for the market is fundamental to that change. It is an ideological belief that private provision is not only cheaper and more efficient but in some way morally superior to public care that is driving change both in health and in the social services. Griffiths has asserted the importance of seeing a growth in private and voluntary provision in welfare, and the partnership between public and private in health care is at the core of the changes now under consideration.

Choice for the consumer is viewed both as a guarantor of standards and a control of costs through competition. Whether that choice is indeed free and unfettered will be examined further in the concluding chapter but the promotion of choice is clearly set to be a keynote of service development for the rest of the century.

The major change in the public sector role can be compared to the approach which the Government has taken to the regeneration of the inner cities. There the traditional role of local government has shifted from one of control to one of facilitation. Instead of local government resources being the instrument driving change, the primary emphasis has been placed on attracting private sector funds to the inner cities and if necessary adjusting regulatory mechanisms to encourage and stimulate the injection of private capital. Local government has, despite initial resistance, shown a remarkable ability to accept this changed world and to release entrepreneurial skills in negotiating the best development packages for local needs. A similar creativity is now sought from managers of welfare services in negotiating from a position of strength as paymasters in putting together acceptable packages of services at local level. The critical issues therefore are to identify differences between the welfare market and the market in property and commercial development, to see what new demands will be placed on service managers by their changed role, and to judge how far the new model of welfare pluralism will succeed in changing existing structures. The logical place to commence that

examination is the United States, where the retreat from public
provision started earlier from a much lower level of public care
and has gone furthest towards a regulatory and standard setting
role.

8
Towards the Twenty-First Century

The United States has a long tradition of welfare pluralism. Despite the growth in public sector funding of welfare programmes, notably in President Johnson's 'Great Society' package, there remained a thriving voluntary sector providing social services often under the banner of religious affiliation or ethnic identity. In addition, there has always been a private for-profit sector offering specialist services on a contract basis to individuals or to public agencies. The same mix can be seen in the United Kingdom. The difference lies in the relative strengths of the private and voluntary sectors which have been a small proportion of total spending in the UK but have provided around 30 per cent of all social welfare spending in the USA.

The past twenty years have seen a radical shift in the American pattern of provision with two major trends identifiable. First, there has been a dramatic expansion of the share of social services provided by public agencies purchasing services from the private and voluntary sector increasing from 25 per cent to 54 per cent between 1971 and 1978 (Kramer and Grossman 1987, p. 33). Secondly, there has been an equally rapid development of the for-profit sector starting with nursing home care of the elderly and then moving into other areas from child care to corrections (the euphemism for prisons).

This shift has been influenced by a drive for greater efficiency in welfare provision. The burgeoning of programmes under the Great Society initiative had been accompanied by waste and duplication, and the advent of the Nixon Administration brought with it a renewed determination to introduce business management

149

methods to social welfare. One way of doing so was to generate a market in social services provision through the emergence of competing service agencies, and increased access to publicly-generated financial support was the precondition for the stimulation of for-profit agencies. Amendments to the Social Security Act in 1974 changed the conditions for public funding of private and voluntary agencies and thus created the conditions for expansion.

In a detailed analysis of purchase of service contracting, Kramer and Grossman quote public officials as offering the following reasons for the decision to use a voluntary or private agency – lower costs, greater flexibility, the specialised and less bureaucratic character of community-based organisations, the ease of starting and terminating programmes, the promotion of choice, volunteerism, innovation, and a better public–private service mix. Once the decision has been taken, the usual process is to draw up what is essentially a tender document specifying 'the particular type and quantity of services needed, the target population to be served, the acceptable cost range, administrative requirements, and procedures for application review' (Kramer and Grossman 1987, p. 35). Sometimes detailed additional conditions about qualifications, access for the handicapped and citizen participation are included. The requests for proposals (RFPs) are thus a clear and highly specific statement of public expectation.

Unlike the building and construction industry, where a number of potential tenderers can readily be identified, the imperfect and fledgling welfare market cannot be relied upon to offer a range of competition. Kramer and Grossman describe three strategies used to manipulate the market: special conferences or workshops to explain what is required; direct assistance to potential providers to help in establishing the necessary organisational structure, whether through the loan of staff or technical assistance like accounting help; and defining service needs so narrowly that competition is effectively limited to a single supplier. In practice public agencies were found to favour the larger, more bureaucratic organisations better equipped to satisfy the procedural steps of the contracting process (Kramer and Grossman 1987, pp. 35–8).

Before considering the ethical issues raised by the introduction of considerations of profit, it is instructive to look at the monitoring mechanisms developed to assess the effectiveness of the services purchased. These were characteristically monthly reports but revealed all the weaknesses evident in monitoring social services programmes in Britain. 'Typically monitors place more emphasis on fiscal than service reporting, and the latter is restricted to outputs (efforts) rather than outcomes (effectiveness). Outcome evaluation is exceedingly rare and infrequently requested. Indeterminant technologies, ambiguous goals (e.g. prevention), and very short time limits are conducive to by-passing the complex issues of effectiveness' (Kramer and Grossman 1987, p. 41).

The validity of monitoring must be questioned in the absence of agreed indicators. The virtues ascribed to a vibrant private and voluntary sector of diversity, cost-efficiency and innovativeness owe more to the preconceptions in the eye of the beholder than to demonstrable evidence.

The application of the profit motive to care affronts the sensibilities of many who would readily accept competition in other areas where the State once occupied a monopolistic position. Even health care seems to be more acceptable as an area for private provision. Gilbert (1983) suggests two reasons for the public distaste for profit in social welfare. First, the intrusion of pecuniary motives in areas of care traditionally delivered by families and motivated by love and affection is felt to be inappropriate, thus differing from health care where specific specialised skills are required beyond the competence of the family. Secondly, the public does not expect profit-orientated agencies to operate in a truly competitive market and thus reacts with suspicion that care interests will be subjugated to financial factors.

Titmuss, in his classic book *The Gift Relationship*, regarded the spirit of altruism and the heightened sense of community as ethical justifications for non-profit organisations in preference to profit-making bodies in blood-bank systems. For Gilbert, however, the superiority of non-profit bodies has to be proved on pragmatic grounds. In the absence of evidence of comparative outcomes between the two, he relies on the superior responsiveness of non-profit organisations to the needs of the community. This is seen, first, in the composition of the management boards of non-profit bodies which contain persons representative of the community; secondly, in the charitable character of non-profit organisations; and thirdly, the absence of the drive to profit affords a safeguard against potential exploitation of the vulnerable.

The categorisation of non-profit organisations includes both statutory and voluntary bodies in the UK context. As in the United States a fluid situation in the mix of services now exists, but it does so in the context of limited professional debate. Cooper, from a unique perspective as Head of the Social Work Service before it was transmuted into the Inspectorate, and service in retirement as Chair of CCETSW, has offered an illuminating view of the respective advantages of statutory, voluntary and private provision of personal social services (Cooper 1988).

The public sector has many virtues. It is accountable, responds to defined needs, and provides a safety net for all citizens. The residual function lowers its public image as does the association of the public sector with social control functions whether of delinquency or mental illness. Cooper suggests that the move to a pluralist model of social care is designed to supplement, substitute for or fill gaps in services needed but no longer affordable. This view is tenable in the context of the past decade but it is more questionable whether the model of partnership envisaged by Griffiths would see voluntary provision in this role as it envisages continued public funding through the purchase of service mechanism.

The implications for coherent social policy concern Cooper, who envisages a problem in securing a sense of direction and control as the role of the private and voluntary sectors increases. In particular, 'the private sector provides what the public is willing and able to pay for rather than what the Government necessarily wants in overall social policy terms. When money is the arbitrator ... the actual direction of policy is weakened. The money is the message becomes in itself a viable policy choice' (Cooper 1988).

The further development of the substitute role for the private and voluntary sectors is likely to lead to the depoliticisation of personal social services (and deunionisation). Cooper warns too that professionalism is threatened through the dissipation of professional workers into a host of smaller employing agencies. That could, however, be the familiar juxtaposition of crisis and opportunity, for the unifying values of the profession would be needed more acutely than ever.

The feasibility of the substitute role will depend on the resource backing made available. While the public sector at present offers a comprehensive range of day domiciliary and residential services from cradle to grave, the private and voluntary sectors tend to be highly specialised. A distinctive client group with specific needs is helpful for a charity seeking to attract attention and funding, but this poses two problems for public policy. First, funding from individuals and trusts is easier to secure for 'popular' groups able to appeal to the emotions. Childrens' charities and those dealing with disabilities, receive more generous support than charities working with delinquents, alcohol-abusers or AIDS sufferers. The public sector is therefore likely to supply a very high proportion of resources generated for less popular groups. Secondly, the non-statutory providers are deployed to meet a specific need, but 'an increased knowledge base which recognises both the distinctiveness of disability and the common human needs attaching to it, the tying up of individual packages of care and the groping steps towards responding to the needs of carers are all indicators that it may be questionable whether scarce resources are best spent in organising round ever more discrete categories' (Cooper 1988).

The Griffiths Report

It is important to see how far the proposals in the Griffiths Report meet some of the doubts and anxieties about welfare pluralism expressed above. The intention of the Report is clearly stated. It is to stimulate the further development of the 'mixed economy' of care, and to change the role of social services authorities to that of arrangers and purchasers of care. The proposals are designed to encourage a proportionate increase in private and voluntary services as distinct from publicly provided services. In what is otherwise a pragmatic and closely argued report, it is surprising to find such a bald statement without accompanying evidence of the superior efficacy of care delivered by the non-statutory sectors. The four gains visualised from this shift in the balance of care are; the widening of choice, flexibility, innovation and competition.

The American evidence indicates that flexibility is a consistent theme. Statutory services are slow to respond to changing needs and the less bureaucratic structures can get services operational more speedily. Innovation is more questionable, for where new approaches to service delivery have been pioneered, notably in child care, it has been in conjunction with public agencies. The most influential innovation of the decade – the Kent Community Care scheme – was entirely within a public sector agency. Competition is a reality only in the area of residential care, where affluence has attracted private providers. Whether the financial structure envisaged by Griffiths would be as attractive to the private sector is more doubtful. The choice available for the service-user is more illusory than real if the user is dependent on publicly provided finance for care. Even in residential settings where the user has a number of homes to choose from, considerations of geography will be the major determinant of choice rather than quality of care.

But if some polite scepticism is justified about the political preferences in evidence in the Report, it would be churlish to ignore the gains that could flow from the new framework set out in Griffiths. First, it provides a clear statement of the responsibilities of local authorities and health authorities. Secondly, it offers a means of drawing together the assessment of need and the financial resources available to meet those needs. Thirdly, by its emphasis on the consumer, it provides a system of care managers and named individuals which should provide both more certainty and more consistency in the arrangements for persons discharged to the community. Fourthly, it avoids the seductive trap of reorganisation with its time-consuming and unproductive disruption. In Griffiths' own words, 'it substitutes for the discredited refuge of imploring collaboration and exhorting action a new requirement that collaboration and action are present normally as a condition for grant. It places responsibility for care clearly within the local community, which – subject to minimum provisions for all sections of the disadvantaged groups – can best determine where money should be spent. It will bolster experiment and innovation at local level by not being prescriptive about organisation' (1988, p. vii).

A formidable array of vested interests are ranged against the implementation of the Griffiths recommendations, an indicator of how difficult it is to make progress in this area. The most significant obstacles will be as follows.

1 The concept of a specific grant will be resisted by local government interests as detracting from the ability of the local community to determine its own spending priorities, and as threatening greater central control.

2 The welfare pluralism central to the Report will be resisted by trade unions and professional interests unable to contemplate the profit nexus in care settings, and seeing in the recommendations a threat to their entrenched positions.

3 The new financial arrangements for residential care will be fought by local government fearing that a transfer of social security funds will be inadequate for the needs to be met, and for very different reasons by private proprietors fearing a reduction in income and tighter controls.

4 The transfer of Community Care grants under the Social Fund will be bitterly resisted by trade union and professional interests as blurring the dividing line between social work and income maintenance.

5 The primacy accorded to social services in designing community care will be challenged by nursing interests, particularly those representing community nursing, and by some if not all health authorities.

Given this powerful array of lobby groups, it is scarcely surprising that the initial reaction of the Government to the report was one of hesitation. Yet as both Griffiths and the Audit Commission acknowledge, 'the one option that is not tenable is to do nothing' (1988, p. vi). Changes will therefore be made and even if some of the more contentious proposals are modified, it seems likely that social care planning and individual case management in a more plural system will dominate the next decade.

Resources

The studied neutrality of Griffiths on resource issues was imposed by the terms of reference under which his inquiry was established. Yet even had that constraint not existed it is questionable whether any clear view would have emerged. One of the major conclusions of the Report was the negative impact of the way in which funds were deployed to impede a comprehensive approach to the planning of community services. 'The system is almost designed to produce patchy performance: good where there happen to be earmarked funds and local goodwill and initiative; poor where, in spite of funds being available, the incentives to plan, prioritise, and organise across the whole field are negligible' (1988, p. 9).

What remains open is the scale of resources which the Government will make available to local authorities for community care. The experience of recent years, with a steep reduction in the share of local government expenditure supported through the Rate Support Grant, has demonstrated that even percentage grants offer no immunity against an administration committed to reduce public spending. However, what is offered by Griffiths is a framework whereby a realistic assessment of the costs of community care can be submitted by local authorities and plans adjusted in the light of actual allocations. At present the fragmentation of responsibility makes that assessment unattainable.

Informal Care

Like the Barclay Report, Griffiths recognises the importance of informal care in the total network of provision, and asserts that 'the first task of publicly provided services is to support and where possible strengthen these networks of carers' (1988, p. 5). Barclay went further and asserted that 'if social work policy and practice were directed more to the support and strengthening of informal networks, to caring for the carers and less to the rescue of casualties when networks fail, it is likely that the necessity for such referrals (to social services departments) would be reduced' (1982, p. 200).

 The rediscovery of informal care has been accompanied by suggestions that the existence of publicly provided welfare services in some way undermines the natural desire of families to care for their vulnerable and dependent members. There never was a golden age when family care was more readily available. There were more people in institutional settings in 1900 than in 1985 despite the demographic and social factors militating against family care.

First, there has been an increase in the size of the elderly population requiring care, particularly of the very elderly, over 80 years old. Secondly, changes in family size have reduced the number of potential carers. Thirdly, increased social and geographical mobility makes it more difficult to sustain family care.

Family care is predominantly care by women, and the main burden of care falls on one individual with only limited support from others in the kinship network and friends (Finch and Groves 1983; Nissel and Bonnerjea 1982; Cecil, Offer and St Leger 1987). The caring role is rarely chosen but arises through force of geographical circumstance or the absence of alternatives. It imposes heavy physical emotional and financial costs on the primary carer. Successive studies have documented an alarming picture of carers whose physical and mental health has been impaired by their caring role (Nissel and Bonnerjea 1982; Kinnear and Graycar 1982).

These needs present a challenge to public services if they are to respond effectively in ways which support informal care. While the pressure on resources is genuine, there is much that could be achieved within existing resource allocations. Cecil, Offer and St Leger (1987) identify three basic needs expressed by the carers in their study – information, continuity and security.

Information is essential. Carers feel and are isolated. They need to know what services are available, what are the eligibility criteria, how to apply, and to have that information made available in an easily accessible form.

Continuity of services and an identifiable contact point with public services are of critical importance. The Griffiths recommendation will help to achieve the named individual with responsibility for coordinating a package of services.

Security about the future is a constant anxiety for carers who worry about their ability to cope if the condition of the person cared for deteriorates. Good practice through Individual Programme Planning should be able to provide a measure of reassurance.

These changes could improve the position, but what the focus on carers illustrates is the poverty of day domiciliary respite and residential services. Real choice is denied to carers who are required to make their needs fit what is on offer by way of services rather than having services tailored to accommodate their needs. Yet unless these resources are directed to support informal care more effectively, the thrust of community care can too easily become exploitation of goodwill and familial obligation.

It is important to recognise that different needs are met by different systems. Informal care is not an undifferentiated pool of neighbourliness and goodwill waiting to be tapped by statutory services. The appropriate response for statutory services demands

a more sophisticated conceptualisation of the spectrum of informal care than is offered by either Barclay or Griffiths. Five responses may be seen in this model of informal care and its relationship to professional inputs.

1 Informal care alone with no professional involvement. This would describe situations where the carer supported by family and friends required no input from professional services other than contact with a GP.

2 Informal care supported indirectly by professional help. This would be seen where the input from social services was limited to creating conditions to aid carers, for instance, by providing practical help with premises or equipment to support a self-help group for carers, or encouraging mutual aid groups.

3 Informal care supplemented by statutory services. This is the model of partnership described by Barclay in which services are orientated to meet the needs of carers. Thus services like day care and respite provision are particularly relevant for carers. The timings of services and the days in the week when services are available too often owe more to organisational requirements than to those of the client. An exception to this pattern is the growth of schemes like Crossroads which aim to deliver home-based relief care at a time when it will be most useful to the carer. It is noteworthy that the voluntary sector was able to respond to the need of carers for a flexible service adaptable to their particular needs more readily than was unionised and stereotyped public sector provision.

4 Informal care as a supplement to the primary care from professional resources. This is most evident in the well-established tradition of volunteer input in domiciliary services like meals on wheels, and in individual volunteer work in residential settings. Other examples are the contribution of youth groups in intermediate treatment programmes and most recently the development of Buddie schemes in providing support to persons with AIDS where these schemes are linked to established patterns of professional help.

5 Professional help alone. This is seen when the needs of the client are such that a specialist skill is required. Thus psychotherapy, clinical counselling and some advocacy work are aspects of practice best delivered by the worker alone. It is, however, a

sad reflection on the failure of much current practice fully to engage community resources that a substantial proportion of referrals dealt with by social services would fall in this last category by default rather than by design.

This categorisation of informal care and its relation to statutory services is based on an analysis developed by Whittaker (1986) in the American context. It highlights both the complexity of informal care and the different skills needed to work effectively in this area. These include skills in identifying supporting and creating networks, in negotiation and in coordination as well as the more familiar social work skills. As the full impact of the Griffiths recommendations takes effect, these are the skills which will be needed by those responsible for putting together packages of care for individuals in the community.

The Implications for Social Work

A careful reading of Griffiths reveals only two references to social workers. Throughout the report social services authorities is the phrase used to describe those responsible for delivering community care. The two references suggest that this may not be an coincidence of wording. They are 'the change in role of social services authorities might also allow them to make more productive use of the management abilities and experience of all their staff, including those who are not qualified social workers' (1988, p. 25) and training for social workers 'will need to give greater emphasis to management skills to reflect the proposed change in emphasis of social services' authorities role' (1988, p. 25).

There are two constructions that can be placed on these words. One is that there need to be some adjustments to training and practice to recognise the stronger managerial element in the social work task in the community, and that some of those engaged in coordinating services will not require a formal social work qualification. The other is that the new role envisaged in designing, organising and purchasing services is so fundamentally different from that currently performed that a wholly different approach is required to which social work has a contribution to make.

The debate in the wake of the Barclay Report was focused by

Hadley and Pinker on the respective merits of community social work and a slimline social work practice based on traditional casework. This was an exaggerated polarisation but it remains a real issue in confronting the challenges posed by the Griffiths Report. In his comment that the recommendations for the changed role of social services authorities were foreshadowed by Barclay, Griffiths is identifying the aspect of social care planning. But he is also recognising that social care planning is not necessarily an exclusive function of professional social work.

While other skills may be called into play in social care planning, Barclay notes that 'only the local authority departments have the responsibility and coverage for coherent social care planning. They need to discover and bring into play the potential self-help, volunteer help, community organisations, voluntary and private facilities that exist' (1982, p. 38).

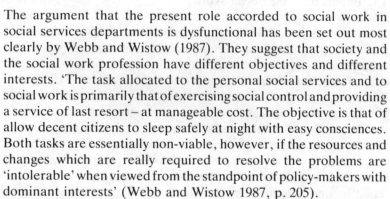

The argument that the present role accorded to social work in social services departments is dysfunctional has been set out most clearly by Webb and Wistow (1987). They suggest that society and the social work profession have different objectives and different interests. 'The task allocated to the personal social services and to social work is primarily that of exercising social control and providing a service of last resort – at manageable cost. The objective is that of allow decent citizens to sleep safely at night with easy consciences. Both tasks are essentially non-viable, however, if the resources and changes which are really required to resolve the problems are 'intolerable' when viewed from the standpoint of policy-makers with dominant interests' (Webb and Wistow 1987, p. 205).

In addition to the mismatch between societal expectations and the aspirations of social work, they contend that the dominant role given to social workers in social services departments in their role of gatekeepers to the allocation of day, domiciliary and residential resources has militated against both the effective organisation of those services and also against a clear and distinctive social work perspective. Thus clients whose needs were primarily practical have received more consideration if they also presented problems requiring counselling help, and social work's advocacy role has been blunted by its location in a large hierarchical structure.

The Seebohm Report, the Barclay Report and, most recently, CCETSW have endorsed a broader view of social work than prevailed in the 1960s. But what Griffiths has endorsed is the philosophy and values of social services departments, not the primacy of social work in delivering community services. Indeed while never making explicit his perception of the social work role. Griffiths may have provided a means of resolving the long-running debate within social work by providing clues to a new structural response to community needs, one which can utilise the categorisation of informal care described above.

A logical organisational response to the issues raised would be to divide the workload into three sections:

(a) A social work service using a variety of counselling skills to work with clients whose primary need is for a therapeutically orientated service. This would apply to the bulk of child care cases, work with people with a mental health problem necessitating clinical counselling or where there is a statutory order, counselling to help adjustment to loss, and so on. The defining characteristic would be the nature of the need presented rather than client category. Work in this section would be focused and often time-limited to maintain a focus on change and adaptation.

The nature of the work would require social workers but the service could buy in specialised skills from the private or voluntary sector. To ensure continuity of service and to ease access there would need to be a cadre of permanent staff, but conceptually there is no reason why the bulk of counselling has to be provided in this way. Provided that strong monitoring is exercised to ensure that clients receive a high quality service the place of employment of the counsellor is irrelevant.

(b) A social care service which would design, organise and, where necessary, purchase services to support vulnerable individuals and their carers. This would include assessment functions in relation to services directly provided by the social services authority, as well as those services provided by the private and voluntary sectors. The primary purpose would be support and maintenance rather than change although, for instance in work with mentally handicapped people, many clients will have a capacity for growth and development.

This service would be influenced by social work values although other professional and non-professional staff would have a major contribution to make to the maintenance task. There would need to be recognition of the importance of responding to changes in knowledge about disability and ageing so that any suggestion of a second-class service could be averted.

(c) A service-planning and evaluation section which would be responsible for contract specifications in negotiations with the private and voluntary sectors. This section would also be charged with performance review, setting objectives for all sections of the organisation. It would set criteria to be met by private contractors. At policy-level, negotiations with health and housing authorities would be focused in this section.

This rudimentary outline appears to offer substantial advantages which meet some of the objections voiced by Webb and Wistow as well as providing a structure better equipped to respond to the Griffiths approach. While it does not address the fundamental issue of the latent conflict between the requirements of policy-makers to keep costs at a manageable level and the scale of expenditure needed to make an impact on the social problems encountered by social services staff, problems likely to be rendered more acute by the consistently regressive impact of fiscal and social security reforms, it does provide a better managerial and organisational context by clarifying roles and responsibilities.

First, it provides a clear distinction between social work and social care, locating social work squarely in the area of change, whether the need for change is defined by the client or defined by virtue of court proceedings. This distinction offers the prospect of improved standards of practice, as it would bring a sharpness of focus and objectives to social work lost in multi-function, multi-client and multi-skill social services departments. It is consistent with the thrust of Pinker's minority note to the Barclay Report. It views social work as a relationship between worker and client in which social workers attempt to help clients whose difficulties are so severe that they threaten their capacity to manage their own lives or to function effectively as members of society, and through use of that relationship assist clients to a better understanding of their problems and their own capabilities to bring about change, if necessary mobilising community resources to facilitate the process of change.

Secondly, it separates the task of social care, accepting that a different mix of skills is needed for this aspect of work. The skills in coordination are not peculiar to social work. It would be a tragedy if territorial rivalries between the professions were to get in the way of effective service delivery but that must be a real danger if social work claims a monopoly of wisdom in this area. The maintenance function has historically been undervalued in social work. Rather than perpetuate the second-class status of social care, a decision to offer a wholly separate service would accord social care functions the importance they deserve. This division would be by far the largest in number and have the bulk of the resources available to social services. The counter-argument deployed against such a split is that 'with a long-term care population requiring frequent reassessment and monitoring, problems arise from an interaction of basic care needs with other difficulties and the need is for a holistic perception of need and the consideration of other solutions to problems' (Davies and Challis 1986, p. 221).

But are social workers the only occupational group able to take a holistic view of need and formulate alternative options? Such a conclusion smacks of professional arrogance and Griffiths appears to hint that there may be other relevant occupations able to contribute to case management.

Thirdly, it offers a clear framework for policy evaluation, monitoring and contract specification – skills which may be possessed by social workers but which are not social work skills. The demands of the new regulatory system with performance objectives for contractors will force agencies to develop negotiating skills more frequently associated with the private sector, in order to secure the best possible price and to ensure compliance with the terms of the contract.

What is important as a unifying theme for these three aspects of the social services task is a coherent set of values underpinning practice. Hitherto it has been argued that 'personal social services have tended to accord too much attention to the production of services, and too little to the provision of service: to the elaboration of what good practice could and should look like' (Webb and Wistow, 1987, p. 232).

The Code of Ethics discussed above provides the basis for the values which are required. Borrowing from concepts derived from industrial and commercial settings of corporate culture and mission statements, a number of social services authorities have set out a clear statement of the principles on which the work of the department is based. These provide staff with clarity about the primary purpose of the organisation and its priorities. A number of common themes emerge from a study of these statements which can in turn identify the key values represented.

One sees here a conjunction of the consumerist emphasis stressed by management gurus like Peters and Waterman (1982) and the new professionalism (discussed in Chapter 4) with its stress on clients' rights. Thus Hertfordshire's statement of departmental philosophy sets out the objectives as:

* doing our best to fit services to the consumer's needs, not the consumer's needs to the service;
* making sure consumers have information about services, and how to gain access to them;
* providing equal access to services irrespective of race, sex or disability;
* giving as much choice as we possibly can to each individual or family;
* listening seriously to what consumers say about us and the services being offered or provided;
* responding as quickly as possible to requests for help and minimising bureaucracy;
* involving consumers in decisions about their lives;
* giving consumers reasons for our decisions.
* treating complaints very seriously;
* making reception a comfortable welcoming experience everywhere;
* meeting the needs of carers and listening to their wishes;
* creating an atmosphere of partnership in all that we do.

(Laming 1988)

This statement reflects the primacy of consumerism as an influence but it also stresses the importance of client participation in decision-making. A similar statement from Derbyshire also emphasises the importance to be attached to what people approve and prefer, but adds a dimension of locality with an assertion that services should 'be local so that people are not removed from their homes or community unless they so choose' (Derbyshire SSD, no date).

As with many statements of aspiration and overarching principle, it is easy to pick holes in this statement, which may be valid in an urban context but is difficult to translate to a rural environment. But what is significant is that now emerging in these statements are the values which underpinned the Seebohm Report twenty years earlier, but tried and tested as of continuing relevance and validity. They reflect explicit statements of the rights of clients in terms of access, participation and complaints procedures; individualised services tailored to user-needs; an emphasis on normalisation and as full a share in the ordinary life of the community as possible; and the provision of locally-based services wherever possible.

The Survival of Social Work

The first paragraph of this book questioned the survival of social work in the chilly waters of the 1990s with sustained right-wing hostility to the role of social workers. As the trends of developments in the organisation, management and location of social work practice have been examined, the resilience of social work in the face of fifteen years of growing public scepticism and even resentment of the social work role is striking. Despite a continuing stream of child-abuse cases touching a raw nerve in the general public, despite the failure to establish or even agree on the desirability of a system of self-regulation, despite the unresolved issues surrounding social work training, and despite the unremitting hostility of the Thatcher government to local government and social welfare programmes, social work is better placed now than in the days before Maria Colwell. That is an extraordinary testimony to the quality of care – often unpublicised – which has been given to millions of people in that period. It is also an eloquent commentary on the ability of the profession to ride the waves of prevailing fashion and preserve its integrity and values. Intake teams, task-centred work, contracts, specialisation, networking, patch, outposting, and resource centres have all had a brief blaze of fashion. Some have been integrated successfully into the mainstream of practice, others have been transmuted to emerge in a new guise and enjoy a surge of popularity all over again. This search for new prescriptions is indicative of some immaturity in a young profession seeking to define its role and contribution, and the tensions between social work, social care and social planning have not been successfully resolved within current structures.

If social work itself is in good heart it is difficult to be so sanguine about social services departments. Politically out of tune with the times, located in a sector of public service which is being progressively stripped of influence and power, and the subject of populist feeling about incompetence and interference, the departments increasingly resemble beached whales threshing about but ultimately doomed. The Griffiths Report has proferred a lifeline but one which the Government is unlikely to extend. Governments have an unhappy tendency to look for structural solutions despite abundant evidence to the contrary. The reorganisation of primary care with responsibility for community care passing to a newly-created primary care authority may be the most likely long-term solution to the dilemma presented by Griffiths.

Whatever the outcome of the deliberations on Griffiths, there will continue to be a need for workers with skills in work with individual groups and communities, the ability to offer assistance and friendship to those who are on the margins of society, and with the ability to marshal a relevant mix of resources to relieve stress and pain. Regardless of the formal qualifications which they may hold, their work needs to be informed and influenced by the principles and values of social work.

Within the ambit of care services, the specific role of qualified social workers may be more narrowly defined than at present but their skills and attitudes will exert a major influence on other aspects of service provision. The practical caring task in what has been termed above 'the social care section' will be discharged by less comprehensively trained staff, possibly at level 2/3 in the NCVQ classification. These staff will build on the work of the home help service to deliver a flexible and individually-designed support service, drawing in, as required, specialised inputs from paramedical nursing or social work staff. Initially the responsibility for organising and managing that service may rest primarily with social workers who already occupy part of that territory – although, as Griffiths comments, the current social work training would need a strengthened managerial component adequately to equip social workers for that role. It is to be hoped that professional barriers will not exclude nursing, paramedical staff and others from moving into the case manager role. At this stage it would be absurd for any single profession to lay exclusive claims to competence in that area.

At a time when continued pressure on welfare expenditure can be expected, it is essential to ensure that resources are used most effectively. That means ensuring that scarce professional skills are used on tasks that only they can perform. The overlapping roles between paramedical nursing and social work staff in community care are wasteful. A narrower definition of the core role for each profession and less restrictive employment practices in those roles, like that of the care manager, which need to draw on a range of skills, would be a more effective use of scarce resources of trained personnel.

The provision of care in the community poses important issues for the professional disciplines involved. Where client interests indicate one worker as the primary worker it will be more difficult to retain the current lines of demarcation which are every bit as real as any shipyard and every bit as counterproductive in impeding the effective delivery of the product (in this case, high-quality care). Already this problem has been encountered in multi-disciplinary community teams, where the roles of community nurses and social workers can rarely be clearly differentiated on paper. This can lead to contests for authority or more positively to a blurring of boundaries and a deliberate subordination of professional identity to the common task.

The Audit Commission quoted approvingly from the Torbay policy document on mental health services: 'the particular professional training is coming to be seen as of less importance than the aptitude for a new style of work. It would be expected that the professional would embrace a truly multi-disciplinary style of working with little emphasis on hierarchy within the centre. This would imply acceptance of equal responsibility with others for the management and development of the centre. . . . Primarily each team member will be seen as a mental health professional' (1986, p. 68). Similar models are evident in community mental handicap teams. While these approaches have the benefit of logic and of riding the tide of customer orientation, it remains to be seen whether this frontal attack on the professions will bear fruit in governmental thinking.

It is unlikely that any of the community-based professional groups would be willing to see their particular contribution diluted, and equally unlikely that any Government would wish to unite those professions in opposition when the support of the professions is critical to the attainment of the policy objectives of more joint working and effective use of limited resources. A safer prophecy would be that there will be more experiments in developing multi-disciplinary teams, that many will fall foul of professional boundary disputes, and that some will elect to resolve those disputes by a model of wholly shared working. Evolution rather than revolution is the more realistic assessment of the changing roles of professionals in community services.

What this chapter has identified is a whole series of question marks about the future. There are doubts about the scope and scale of welfare pluralism, doubts about the reality of current DSW proposals and doubts about the validity of current dividing lines between professions working in the community. Yet there remains an optimism in what is still a young profession – an optimism which sometimes expresses itself almost as arrogance in denigrating the contribution of other disciplines – that it can deliver a better quality of life for hundreds of thousands whose lives are stunted by deprivation, both emotional and physical. Tempered by realism, the social worker's rule of optimism is both a necessary defence mechanism and also the basis for improving services in the constant quest to look for new and better ways of delivering care.

In a society where the gaps between the haves and have-nots have widened and continue to widen with the creation of a new underclass deliberately cast as the losers in a restructuring of social security and employment policy, the social policy role of social work is going to be of major importance. It has the task of alleviating the worst effects of deprivation and inequality and the responsibility of drawing to public attention the social consequences of the measures taken. Fulfilling that latter responsibility may be politically unpopular but it is at the heart of social work in a tradition dating back to Victorian reformers. For the values of care represented by social work, like those of nursing in the clinical context, have a depth and validity which will outlast the contemporary obsessions with cost. There is danger in knowing the price of everything but the value of nothing. Values may be threatened by the fragmentation and financial orientation of the plural welfare structure indicated by Griffiths. Social services authorities and the profesional bodies alike have a vitally important role in ensuring that the new pattern of services reflects a continuity of values, even if in very different organisational settings.

The contribution which social work will make to personal social services provision to the turn of the century may not be the all-embracing service from cradle to grave that the Seebohm Committee envisaged over twenty years ago. That in turn was very different in concept and orientation from the role accorded to social work (even if not designated as such) in the social legislation of 1948. And if in 2008 a Committee reports with recommendations about the future pattern of services it will doubtless address the defects and deficiencies of welfare pluralism. Change is inevitable, and the pace of change is accelerating. That will pose challenges for training in equipping staff to respond positively to new tasks and new settings. But in all the changes one can discern a striking theme of continuity from Seebohm to Barclay to Griffiths.

That continuity lies in the duality of concern for social policy and social planning on the one hand and for individuals and groups in need of care on the other. It is seen in the continuing emphasis on the community and the support which it can offer to supplement the input of the professional helper. It is evident in the stress on the maximum possible participation of citizens in decisions which affect them, and in the desire to bridge the gap between social workers and their clients. Each of those issues remains valid today. Social work may not achieve the full professional status of complete self-regulation and the General Social Work Council, but it can ensure that the issues which have dominated its thinking for the last twenty years remain at the forefront of public and professional concern.

Bibliography

J. Algie, A. Hey and G. Mallen (1981), 'Cuts – Getting Your Priorities Right', *Community Care*, 6 August.

J. Algie and C. Miller (1976), 'Deciding Social Services Priorities', *Social Work Today*, 5 and 19 February.

Association of Directors of Social Services (1986), *Registration and a Social Work Council* (Reading: ADSS).

Auckland Report (1975), *Report of the Committee of Inquiry into the Provision and Coordination of Services to the Family of J. G. Auckland* (London: HMSO).

Audit Commission (1986), *Making a Reality of Community Care* (London: HMSO).

T. Bamford (1976), 'Priorities in the Social Services' in *Social Work Today*, 27 May.

T. Bamford (1982), *Managing Social Work* (London: Tavistock).

Barclay Report (1982), *Social Workers: their Role and Tasks* (London: Bedford Square Press).

H. M. Bartlett (1970), *The Common Base of Social Work Practice* (New York: National Association of Social Workers).

M. Bayley (1982), 'Helping Care to Happen in the Community' in A. Walker (ed.), *Community Care* (London: Basil Blackwell and Martin Robertson).

Beckford Report (1985). *A Child in Trust* (London: Borough of Brent).

W. Bennis and B. Nannis (1985), *Leaders* (New York: Harper and Row).

F. Biestek (1961), *The Casework Relationship* (London: Allen and Unwin).

A. Bovaird and I. Mallinson (1988), 'Setting Objectives and Measuring Achievement in Social Care' in *British Journal of Social Work*, Vol. 18, no. 3, June, pp. 309–23.

J. Bradshaw and I. Gibbs (1988), *Needs and Charges: A Study of Public Support for Residential Care* (Aldershot: Gower).

C. Brewer and J. Lait (1980), *Can Social Work Survive?* (London: Temple Smith).

British Association of Social Workers (1975), *A Code of Ethics* (Birmingham: BASW).

British Association of Social Workers (1976) *The Relationship between Field and Residential Social Work* (Birmingham: BASW).

British Association of Social Workers (1977), *The Social Work Task* (Birmingham: BASW).

British Association of Social Workers (1980), *Clients are Fellow Citizens* (Brimingham: BASW).

British Association of Social Workers (1983), *Effective and Ethical Recording* (Birmingham: BASW).

British Assocation of Social Workers (1988), *Complaints Procedures in Social Work* (Birmingham: BASW).

Butler-Sloss Report (1988), *Report of the Inquiry into Child Abuse in Cleveland 1987* (London: HMSO).

Z. Butrym (1976), *The Nature of Social Work* (London: Macmillan).

P. Bywaters (1986), 'Social Work and The Medical Profession – Arguments Against Unconditional Collaboration', *British Journal of Social Work*, Vol. 16, no. 6, December).

R. Cecil, J. Offer and F. St. Leger (1987), *Informal Welfare* (Aldershot: Gower).

Central Council for Education and Training in Social Work (1973), *Setting the Course for Social Work Education 1971–1973* (London: CCETSW).

Central Council for Education and Training in Social Work (1973), *Training for Residential Work* (London: CCETSW).

Central Council for Education and Training in Social Work (1974), *Residential Work is Part of Social Work* (London: CCETSW).

Central Council for Education and Training in Social Work (1975), *Guidelines for Post-Qualifying Studies*, mimeograph (London: CCETSW).

Central Council for Education and Training in Social Work (1975), *Principles, Procedures and Criteria for the Approval of Post-qualifying Studies*, mimeograph (London: CCETSW).

Central Council of Education and Training in Social Work (1983), *Review of Qualifying Training Policy*, Report of the Council Working Group Paper 20.1 (London: CCETSW).

Central Council for Education and Training in Social Work (1985) *Policies for Qualifying Training: Report on Consultation* (London: CCETSW).

Central Council for Education and Training in Social Work (1987), *Perspectives in Training for Residential Work* (London: CCETSW).

Central Council of Education and Training in Social Work (1987a), *Care for Tomorrow* (London: CCETSW).

D. Challis and E. Ferlie (1987), 'Changing Patterns of Fieldwork Organisation, I and II' in *British Journal of Social Work*, April, pp. 147–66.

J. Cheetham (1982), *Social Work Services for Ethnic Minorities in Britain and the USA* (London: DHSS).

Colwell Report (1974), *Report of the Committee of Inquiry into the Care and Supervision Provided in Relation to Maria Colwell* (London: HMSO).

J. Cooper (1983), *The Creation of the British Personal Social Services* (London: Heinemann).

J. Cooper (1988), 'The Mosaic of Personal Social Services' in *British Journal of Social Work*, Vol. 18, no. 3, June.

P. Corrigan and P. Leonard (1978), *Social Work Practice Under Capitalism* (London: Macmillan).

V. Coulshed (1988), *Social Work Practice: An Introduction* (London: Macmillan/BASW Practical Social Work).

Court Report (1976), *Fit for the Future: Report of the Committee on Child Health Services* (London: HMSO).

R. Currie and B. Parrott (1986), *A Unitary Approach to Social Work: Application in Practice*, 2nd ed. (Birmingham: British Assocation of Social Workers).

J. Cypher (1986), 'Citizenship and the New Professionalism' in *Social Work and Citizenship*, ed. S. Etherington (Birmingham: BASW).

B. Davies and D. Challis (1986), *Matching Resources to Needs in Community Care* (Aldershot: Gower).

M. Davies (1981), *The Essential Social Worker* (London: Heinemann).

M. Davies and J. Brandon (1979), 'The Limits of Competence in Social Work' in *British Journal of Social Work*, Vol. 9, no. 3, Autumn.

Department of Health and Social Security (1971), *Better Services for the Mentally Handicapped*, Cmnd 4683 (London: HMSO).

Department of Health and Social Security (1974), Circular LA(74)(36), *Rate Fund Expenditure and Rate Calls in 1975/76* (London: HMSO).

Department of Health and Social Security (1975), *Better Services for the Mentally Ill*, Cmnd 6233 (London: HMSO).

Department of Health and Social Security (1976), *Priorities for Health and Personal Social Services* (London: HMSO).

Department of Health and Social Security (1976), *Manpower and Training for the Social Services* (London: HMSO).

Department of Health and Social Security (1977), *Joint Care Planning: Health and Local Authorities*, Circular HC (77)17/LAC(77)10 (London: HMSO).

Department of Health and Social Security (1979), *Report of the Royal Commission of the Health Service*, Cmnd 7615 (London: HMSO).

Department of Health and Social Security (1981), *Care in Action*, (London: HMSO).

Department of Health and Social Security (1981), *Care in the Community: A Consultative Document on Moving Resources for Care in England*, HC (81)9/LAC(81)5 (London: DHSS).

Department of Health and Social Security (1981), *Growing Older*, Cmnd 8173 (London: HMSO).

Department of Health and Social Security (1983), *Personal Social Services Records – Disclosure of Information to Clients*, LAC(83) (London: DHSS).

Department of Health and Social Security (1988), *Report of the Inquiry into Child Abuse in Cleveland 1987*, Cmnd 413 (London: HMSO).

R. Dworkin (1977), *The Philosophy of Law* (Oxford: Oxford University Press).

H. Fayol (1916), *General and Industrial Management* (London: Pitman).

J. Finch and D. Groves (eds) (1983), *A Labour of Love: Women, Work and Caring* (London: Routledge & Kegan Paul).

Firth Report (1987), *Public Support for Residential Care: Report of Working Party* (London: DHSS).

J. Fischer (1976), *The Effectiveness of Social Casework* (New York: Charles C. Thomas).

M. S. Folkard (1975), *Impact*, Vol. 1, Home Office Research Study no. 24 (London: HMSO).

M. S. Folkard (1976), *Impact*, Vol. 2, Home Office Research Study no. 36 (London: HMSO).

W. Francis (1987), 'Setting the Wheels in Motion', *Community Care*, 27 August.

N. Gilbert (1983), *Capitalism and the Welfare State* (New Haven: Yale University Press).

H. Giller and A. Morris (1981), *Care and Discretion* (London: Burnett Books).

E. M. Goldberg and R. W. Warburton (1979), *Ends and Means in Social Work* (London: Allen and Unwin).

H. Goldstein (1973), *Social Work Practice: A Unitary Approach* (Columbia, South Carolina: University of South Carolina Press).

Griffiths Report (1983) *NHS Management Inquiry* (London: DHSS).

Griffiths Report (1988), *Community Care: Agenda for Action* (London: HMSO).

R. Hadley and S. Hatch (1981), *Social Welfare and the Failure of the State* (London: Allen and Unwin).

R. Hadley and M. McGrath (1980), *Going Local: Neighbourhood Social Services* (London: Bedford Square Press).

R. Hadley and M. McGrath (1984), *When Social Services are Local: the Normanton Experience* (London: Allen and Unwin).

P. Hall (1976), *Reforming the Welfare* (London: Heinemann).

P. Halmos (1965), *The Faith of the Counsellors* (London: Constable).

M. Horne (1987), *Values in Social Work* (Aldershot: Wildwood House, Community Care Practice Handbook).

House of Commons Social Services Committee, 1984/85 session, Second Report (1985), *Community Care with Special Reference to Adult Mentally Ill and Mentally Handicapped People* (London: HMSO).

E. Humphreys (1987), 'A Sharing Experience in Social Services', *Insight*, 28 August.

P. Jenkin (1980), Speech to Age Concern, 7 February.

Joint Steering Group on Accreditation, Second and Final Report (1980), (Birmingham: BASW).

C. Jones (1983), *State Social Work and the Working Class* (London: Macmillan).

B. Jordan (1984), *Invitation to Social Work* (Oxford: Basil Blackwell).

B. Jordan (1987), 'Counselling Advocacy and Negotiation', *British Journal of Social Work*, vol. 17, no. 2.

Kimberly Carlisle Report (1987), *A Child in Mind* (London Borough of Greenwich).

D. King and M. Court (1984), 'A Sense of Scale' in *Health and Social Services Journal*, 21 June.

Kings Fund (1987), *Facilitating Innovation in Community Care* (London: Kings Fund).

D. Kinnear and A. Graycar (1982), *Family Care of Elderly People: Australian Perspectives* (Kensington, NSW: Social Welfare Centre).

M. Kogan and J. Terry (1971), *The Organisation of a Social Service Department: A Blueprint* (London: Bookstall Publications).

R. Kramer and B. Grossman (1987), 'Contracting for Social Services: Process Management and Resource Dependencies' in *Social Service Review*, no. 61, pp. 32–55.

H. Laming (1988), 'Corporate Identity' in *Social Services Insight*, 8 April.

C. S. Levy (1973), 'The Value Base of Social Work' in *Journal of Education for Social Work*, no. 9, pp. 34–42.

R. K. Merton (1968), *Social Theory and Social Structure* (New York: Free Press).

J. Moore (1986), 'Citizenship – Social Work and Women' in *Social Work and Citizenship*, ed. S. Etherington (Birmingham: BASW).

E. Murphy (1987), 'Community Care I: Problems' in *British Medical Journal*, 12 December.

E. Murphy (1988), 'Community Care II: Possible Solutions' in *British Medical Journal*, 2 January.

N. Murray (1987), 'Going Local?' in *Social Services Insight*, 10 April.

J. Naisbitt (1982), *Megatrends* (New York: Warner).

National Consumer Council and National Institute for Social Work (1988), *Open to Complaints* (London: National Consumer Council).

National Development Group for the Mentally Handicapped (1977), *Mentally Handicapped Children* (London: DHSS).

M. Nissel and L. Bonnerjea (1982), *Family Care of the Handicapped Elderly: Who Pays?* (London: Policy Studies Institute).

R. Parker (1981), 'Tending and Social Policy' in *A New Look at the Personal Social Services*, eds M. Goldberg and S. Hatch (London: Policy Studies Institute).

C. Parker and S. Etherington (1987), in *Social Services Insight*, 21 August.

P. Parsloe (1981), *Social Services Area Teams* (London: Allen and Unwin).

P. Parsloe and O. Stevenson (1978), *Social Services Teams: The Practitioner's Task* (London: HMSO).

M. Payne (1982), *Working in Teams* (London: Macmillan).

Personal Social Services Council (1975), *Living and Working in Residential Homes* (London: PSSC).

T. Peters and R. Waterman (1982), *In Search of Excellence* (New York: Harper and Rowe).

A. Pincus and A. Minahan (1973), *Social Work Practice: Model and Method* (Ithaca, Illinois: Peacock).

S. Rees (1978), *Social Work Face to Face* (London: Edward Arnold).

W. Reid and L. Epstein (1972), *Task Centred Casework* (New York: Columbia University Press).

W. Reid and A. Shyne (1969), *Brief and Extended Casework* (New York: Columbia University Press).

M. Rhodes (1986), *Ethical Dilemmas in Social Work Practice*, (London: Routledge & Kegan Paul).

C. Rogers (1953), 'The Characteristics of a Helping Relationship' in *Personnel and Guidance Journal*, no. 37.

R. Rowbottom, A. Hey and D. Billis (1974), *Social Services Departments: Developing Patterns of Work and Organisation* (London: Heinemann).

Royal Commission on the National Health Service (1979) (London: HMSO).

Seebohm Report (1968), *Report of the Committee on Local Authority and Allied Personal Social Services*, Cmnd 3703 (London: HMSO).

B. Sheldon (1986), 'Social Work Effectiveness Experiments: Review and Implications' in *British Journal of Social Work*, April, Vol. 16, pp. 223–42.

M. Simpkin (1983), *Trapped within Welfare*, 2nd edn (London: Macmillan).

Social Services Committee, 1984/1985 session, Second Report (1985), *Community Care with Special Reference to Adult Mentally Ill and Mentally Handicapped People* (London: HMSO).

H. Specht and A. Vickery (1977), *Integrating Social Work Methods* (London: George Allen & Unwin, National Institute Social Services Library no. 31).

Standing Conference of Organisations of Social Workers (1965), Discussion Paper 1.

O. Stevenson (1981), *Specialisation in Social Service Teams* (London: George Allen & Unwin).

M. Thatcher (1981), Speech to Women's Royal Voluntary Service, reported in *Community Care*, 29 January.

P. Townsend (1970), 'The Objectives of the New Social Service' in *The Fifth Social Service* (London: Fabian Society).

Tyra Henry Report (1987), *Whose Child? Report into the Death of Tyra Henry* (London Borough of Lamlett).

A. Vickery (1977), *Caseload Management*, National Institute for Social Work Paper no. 5 (London: National Institute for Social Work).

Wagner Report (1988), *Residential Care – A Positive Choice* (London: HMSO).

A. Webb and G. Wistow (1987), *Social Work, Social Care and Social Planning: The Personal Social Services Since Seebohm* (London: Longman).

Welsh Office (1983), *All-Wales Strategy for the Development of Service for Mentally Handicapped People* (Cardiff: Welsh Office).

P. Westland (1987), 'How Many Hats Can Ms Fixit Wear?' in *Social Services Insight*, 10 July.

R. Whitmore and R. Fuller (1980), 'Priority Planning in an Area Team' in *British Journal of Social Work*, Vol. 10, no. 3.

J. Whittaker (1986), 'Integrating Formal and Informal Social Care: A Conceptual Framework' in *British Journal of Social Work*, Vol. 16, Supplement.

B. Wooton (1959), *Social Science and Social Pathology* (London: George Allen & Unwin).

E. Younghusband (1978), *Social Work in Britain: 1950–1975*, Vols 1 and 2 (London: George Allen & Unwin).

Index